The Other Side of Jordan
and
Other Full Length Plays

(Book One)

S AMUEL W ILLIAMS

PARTRIDGE
A Penguin Random House Company

Copyright © 2014 by Samuel Williams.

ISBN: Softcover   978-1-4828-9591-9
            Ebook   978-1-4828-9263-5

All rights reserved. No part of this book may be used or reproduced by any means, graphic, electronic, or mechanical, including photocopying, recording, taping or by any information storage retrieval system without the written permission of the publisher except in the case of brief quotations embodied in critical articles and reviews.

Because of the dynamic nature of the Internet, any web addresses or links contained in this book may have changed since publication and may no longer be valid. The views expressed in this work are solely those of the author and do not necessarily reflect the views of the publisher, and the publisher hereby disclaims any responsibility for them.

To order additional copies of this book, contact
Toll Free 800 101 2657 (Singapore)
Toll Free 1 800 81 7340 (Malaysia)
orders.singapore@partridgepublishing.com

www.partridgepublishing.com/singapore

CONTENTS

A NOTE FROM THE AUTHOR

These plays have been written as much for teaching as for enjoyment. While many may relate and relegate them to a specific group or location, as the author of them all, I would readily confront this mischaracterization of their contents, reach and intent. Their messages are universal and their applications are timeless. There is much more to them than meets the eye. I sincerely hope that you will enjoy them yet take from them their true intents and purposes.

SPECIAL ACKNOWLEDGEMENTS

Any time a book such as this is written, without question there are many people to whom special recognitions are due. As such I would like to recognize:

God: For your motivation, inspiration, insight and gifting to complete this task.

Sharleen (My wife): For being that constant support system and for granting me the time and space required to accomplish this task.

Samuel and Shundalynn (Our children): For your inspiration, motivation, support and faith in me.

Ruby Williams (My mother): For your constant love, support and listening ear.

Geraldine, Bevelyn, Joanne, Patricia and Sonya (My sisters): For all the prayers, support, confidence and love each of you show me every day of my life.

Rev (Dr.) Christopher Lowe (Friend and mentor): For being that spiritual brother and advisor that I definitely needed.

I would like to also recognize the individuals whose lives inspired me to write the plays which appear in this four volume series. Thank you for sharing a deeply private and protected part of yourselves with me. I pray that I have done your experiences justice in this series.

BEHOLD EMMANUEL

The Christmas Story
(Part 1)

A Miracle In Every Way is a two-part play with both parts being full length in duration. Each part can be performed independently, but, when and if possible, should be performed in unison. Contained in this book, however, is only the first half of the play which has been entitled "Behold Immanuel".

NARRATOR #1

(Now) When there was nothing at all—not even time—God spoke, and by the word of His power, He created everything.

NARRATOR #2

For by Him all things were created that are in heaven and that are upon the earth, visible and invisible, whether thrones or dominions or principalities or powers. All things were created through Him and for Him. And He is before all things, and in Him all things consists.

NARRATOR #1

He spoke!!!

NARRATOR #2

And the heavenly host appeared.

NARRATOR #1

And though there stood before Him all angelic beings, the magnificent El Shadai saw the need to separate them into distinct and dutiful divisions. One division He called the Warriors, another He called His Messengers, and the other He identified as His worshippers.

NARRATOR #2

Each division was led by an appointed archangel. Gabriel was the God—appointed leader of the Messenger Angels. Michael was appointed to lead the Warring or Fighting Angels. And strikingly handsome Lucifer was set over God's very own Worshipping Angels. How beautiful Lucifer was. For God had created his very unique and special appearance to reflect the preciousness of his position in God's kingdom and to God's own heart—the chief of worship, the essence of praise and worship. How special and sacred was Lucifer and his duties in the heart of God. (Opens his garment to chimes and the forceful singing of angels.) For, you see, at this time the kingdom of God had no adversaries, and, therefore, the warring angels had no enemies against whom to fight, and the messenger angels had no one to whom to carry God's messages. Therefore, only the worshippers truly served their designated purpose—at this time.

NARRATOR #1

This, of course, made Lucifer very happy, and as a result he became so filled with pride and arrogance that he actually asked God . . .

LUCIFER

(To God) Oh Great and Marvelous Jehovah, I have come into your presence to seek your permission to gather the praises of all your angelic hosts unto myself, then I shall offer up their collective praises to You on behalf of all your angels. For surely Gabrielle's messenger angels have no missions. For to whom is there for them to carry a message from you? In the whole of Your creation there is nothing but angels . . . and we all are here in your very presence. There is no need for such creatures other than to give praises and worship unto You—(proudly) as do MY worshipping angels. And Michael . . . Your chief angelic warrior . . . who hath he to fight? For shall one angel battle against another? Certainly not!! Likewise, the Warriors too serve no purpose in your creation but to praise as we do. For the heavens are set ablaze with

Your power and glory when my angels and I bless You with the fruit of our lips. Therefore, how much more will we bless You if You should command the others to submit their worship to my angels and me. Then ALL the heavenly host will be under my command and power. And they will kneel before me. And they will surrender their worship unto me and I will collect all of the worship of Your creatures and will bring it before You as a sweet savor, and I will present these praises unto You as the worship of your angelic hosts.

VOICE

Lucifer, thou heart is full of pride and iniquity. It is because this is so that I have found the need to create the other angels.

LUCIFER

Why hath thou done this creation, God? Is not the intent of my heart perfect in your sight?

VOICE

Thine heart is far from perfect, Lucifer and the iniquities hidden therein have made need of the full creation of the heavenly host.

LUCIFER

Mine heart? But only to worship You is the desire of my heart.

VOICE

The words of your lips and the meditations of your heart are at war one with the other, Lucifer. Be not deceived, nor shall any bow down to worship you. I and I alone am God and beside Me there is no other. I am a jealous God and will share my glory with no other.

LUCIFER

To whom, then, shall the warring and messenger angels give their worship? And what is hidden in my heart that you would find need to create them?

VOICE

At the sound of My name, Lucifer, every knee shall bow and every tongue shall confess in true praise and worship that I and I alone am God, each for himself and out of the abundance of his own heart. Your heart is filled with pride, deceit, lies, greed, lust for power, strife, selfishness and all that is evil, Lucifer. Though created by Me to worship, your worship is as useless noise before my throne. It is neither pure nor true. This is why I have created the other angels.

LUCIFER

(Emotional and angry) It shall not be!! They shall not share my glory! Worship is mine to give and to receive! I am the worshipping king! I am the archangel of music and praise! I am beautifully created so that I may render praise unto God myself— NOT them!! No warring angel—no messenger angel—no other creation can do what I do! None!! I am Lucifer the great!! (To his fellow worshipping angels) And, yes, I do speak out of the secrets of my heart. Yes I shall over throw HIM from his own throne! And yes I shall take over the heavens! And Yes I shall exalt myself high above other creations just as God Himself is!! And I—I—Lucifer shall be as God Himself!! Then I shall be worshipped! And praised! And glorified! And exalted! For I shall be as El Shadai Himself!! Yes! Yes! It shall be so!! ANGELS PREPARE FOR BATTLE!! PREPARE TO CONQUER THE HEAVENS AND EXALT ME AS YOUR KING AND GOD!!

GABRIEL

Angels! Prepare for battle! (All angels under his command draw their swords and prepare for battle.)

MICHAEL

Angels! Prepare for battle! (All angels under his command draw their swords and prepare for battle.)

LUCIFER

Angels!! Attack and destroy them all!! Attack them! Attack them! Atta-c-k-k-k-k them!!

NARRATOR #1

Then a great war of the spirits broke out in the heavens. It was a war which saw God's own angels battle one against the other. The Lucifer-led worshippers engaged in fierce battle against the Michael-led warring angels and the Gabriel-led messenger angels. And when the battle was over, Lucifer and his followers—one third of God's heavenly host—were soundly defeated and casted out of heaven.

NARRATOR #2

But God's heart was much saddened, for His very own creation—His worshipping angels—had turned against Him. Though God still had His warring angels . . . and though He still had his messenger angels, there was a yet a void in His heart, and there now were no more worshippers in all the heaven.

NARRATOR #1

Then God decided to create a new worshipper. He decided to make a man—in His own image and in His own likeness.

(Off stage reading and on-stage enactment of "The Creation" by James Weldon Johnson. Permission to reprint this poem in its entirety was not received from its author.

And God stepped out on space, and He looked around and said, "Im lonely, I'll make me a world." . . . This Great God, Like a mammy bending over her baby, kneeled down in the dust toiling over a lump of clay till He shaped it in His own image; Then into it He blew the breath of life, and man became a living soul. Amen.

LIGHTS

SCENE II

(Setting: The Garden of Eden. Action opens with Adam and Eve receiving divine instructions from the voice of God.)

VOICE

Of every tree in the garden you may eat except the tree which is in the center of the garden which is the tree of the knowledge of good and evil, life and death. And of its fruits, you may not eat. For surely the day that you shall eat thereof, you shall surely die. I have given unto you power, wisdom, authority and dominion over all created things, whether they be fish, beast, powers, dominions, angels or principalities. You have been given My likeness and My image. You are to rule over the earth just as I rule over the heavens. And no other god shall you have before Me. Go forth! Subdue all things. Bring them under your dominion. And replenish the earth. This is My will for you upon the earth. But remember!! Of the tree of knowledge of good and evil, you are NEVER to eat. For the day that you eat of it . . . surely . . . SURELY . . . you . . . shall . . . die!!

NARRATOR #2

And God's presence departed from the Garden of Eden. And in came Lucifer in the form of a serpent. (Enters Lucifer in the form of huge cunning yet friendly serpent.)

NARRATOR #1

Now the serpent was more cunning than any beast of the field. He spoke with Eve concerning the fruit of the tree of life. And Eve saw that it was good and pleasant to behold. And the serpent tempted her, for in that day the whole earth spoke but one language—even the animals.

SERPENT

(He notices Eve who is hard at work picking the fruit and attending the garden. Then to himself . . .) Eve . . . Eve . . . I have patiently sought you for such a time as this. (He casually and carefully reveals himself to Eve who initially appears mildly shocked at his presence, but quickly adjusts and engages the deceptive creature in a brief conversation. To Eve . . .) Behold how beautiful the fruit of the tree of life appears.

EVE

Oh yes. They are exceedingly pleasant to behold.

SERPENT

And to touch?

EVE

(Eve casually touches a fruit on the tree.) Hm-m-m. It is also pleasant to touch.

SERPENT

A-a-n-n-d . . . to taste?

EVE

(Appearing surprised that he would ask her such a question.) To taste? How would I know this? For God has spoken unto us, and has told us that surely we shall die the day we eat of the fruit of this tree.

SERPENT

And His word you have received and believed in your heart?

EVE

This is true. I have done this thing which you have just said. Have not you done the same?

SERPENT

(Beguilingly) Yes. Yes. I have done the same.

EVE

Serpent, why hath thou not spoken to Adam, my man?

SERPENT

(To himself) For I know the commitment of his heart toward his God and that I cannot sway him. (To Eve) uh-h-h. I will speak with him now. Where is this . . . Adam?

EVE

He is there, caring for the garden as he was told.

(Lucifer crosses toward Adam yet ensures to remain out of Adam's sight. He notices Eve's glance and feigns a conversation with Adam via gestures. He makes eye contact with Eve, waves to her to ensure she observes his and Adam's "conversation" then returns cross stage to Eve.)

SERPENT

I have spoken with your man and have found him to be a creature of great pleasure. (Eve smiles) Like you, he also says that the fruits of the tree of life are good to behold . . . and to touch . . . and to taste too. And were he not busy, he would himself taste of these beautiful and tender fruits.

EVE

This is what he has said?

SERPENT

But of course, Eve.

EVE

How hast thou known my name?

SERPENT

I know much, Eve. I have lived before there was time. I have been here in the garden in your mist for countless years and have heard your talks with Adam and your conversations with God during the cool of the day. I know who you are, Eve. I even know who you are in your heart.

EVE

This is so? Why hath thou done such a thing? To spy upon us?

SERPENT

Because I have sought you, Eve and now proclaim like a roaring lion, that this day, I have captured my prey.

EVE

(Confused.) Prey? Roaring lion? (Shrugs it off) How then may I call you? (Laughingly) A lion or a serpent?

SERPENT

Lion? Serpent? No!! I am Lucifer. I am a fallen angel. I am he who was exalted but am now no more. I have known God and have sat in His very presence. For I once was His chief worshipper.

EVE

And doth thou yet worship my God, the God of the heavenly host?

SERPENT

Indeed not woman!! For I rose against Him and challenged His power . . . and was defeated and casted down from his presence.

EVE

And now?

SERPENT

I am defeated and cast down and away from His presence. But this one thing I learned while in His presence.

EVE

What might this thing be, Lucifer?

SERPENT

The secret of His power . . . His might . . . His majestic presence . . . of HIM!! I know God's secret!! And I can make you just as HE is. If only you will to do as I say. Surely I shall make you as God Himself.

EVE

If thou hast power to do this deed of which you speak, why hast thou not done this very deed for yourself? Why hast thou then not made yourself as God? Then you would not have been defeated.

SERPENT

Uu-u-u-uggg! Such questions I do hate!!

EVE

Certainly, thou hast no power no authority to do this thing which thou boast of.

SERPENT

A-a-h-h. This is true. *I* have neither the power nor authority to do this thing . . . but *YOU* do. For the power to do this thing was left with you.

EVE

With me even?

SERPENT

(Retrieving a fruit from the forbidden tree.) Yes! It is here . . . in the fruit of the tree of knowledge.

EVE

The fruit?

SERPENT

Of this tree only. And when you have eaten of it, then shall your eyes be made open . . . and then shall you become as God Himself!

EVE

But God has forbidden that we should eat of the fruit of this tree. And only this tree. How be it then that you say our power to become as God lies in our disobedience to His word?

SERPENT

Because He is a jealous God and will not share His power and glory with none other. He has forbidden you to eat of this tree because He knows that the day you eat of it, you too shall be as He is. You too shall be God. And there shall be none other mightier than yourself!

EVE

Serpent, of this thing you are sure?

SERPENT

Of this one thing I am most sure, and I promise you will not only discover the truth about God, but you will also discover the truth of my words as well. Now eat, Eve, and behold yourself as God. Eat! Eat!

NARRATOR #1

Eve then took the fruit and ate of it and took it to Adam to share it with him.

EVE

I have done as you had wished to do but were too busy?

ADAM

(Still tending the garden.) And what might that be, Eve?

EVE

I have eaten from the tree in the center of the garden. As you told the serpent you wished to do (Adam is astonished).

ADAM

Eve!! What is this thing you have done? I have spoken of no such desire to you, a serpent or any other beast of the field.

EVE

(Pointing to the laughing serpent) But he said . . .

ADAM

Never mind what he said. What did God say to us, Eve?

EVE

But the serpent said we would not die if we ate of the tree . . . .

ADAM

And is he wiser than our God?

EVE

(Rebelliousness can be heard in her voice and observed in her antics. Sin has entered her spirit.) The serpent said I would live. God said I would die. Do I not yet live, Adam? Do I or do I not?

ADAM

(Adam observes her momentarily then reluctantly concedes . . .) You do yet live, Eve.

EVE

Who then do you say is smarter . . . our jealous God . . . . or the wise serpent? Eat Adam . . . and become one with the serpent and me. Eat and become wiser than God Himself. (Pointing to herself as proof) Surely you shall not die. Eat of the forbidden tree and become as God himself. (Forcefully offering the fruit to Adam who eventually and reluctantly receives it and begins to eat of it.) Eat! Eat!

NARRATOR #2

Adam received the fruit from Eve and ate of it also. And Satan rejoiced. For he had deceived God's greatest creation and had gained legal rights into the earth realm as its god. Adam and Eve had traded their God-likeness for a piece of fruit. They were ashamed and fled to seek leaves to cover their nakedness; and Satan was now the prince of this world. For through their rebelliousness toward God, they relinquished all of man's divine rights, powers and authorities to Lucifer.

LUCIFER

Ha! Ha! Ha! Ha! Ha! Ha! Ha! Now I shall reign as the god of this world forever. I shall steal, kill, and destroy His every good and perfect creation. No good thing shall I not seek to destroy. For I am the god of this world now. All creations will see me as I promised. I shall exalt my throne high above the stars and I shall appear as God Himself. And Yes!! Every knee shall bow and every tongue shall confess that I Lucifer am Lord of Lord, King of Kings, and I that I am above even El Elyon Himself! HA! HAA! HA! HA! HAA!

VOICE

It shall not be so!! This I shall not suffer to be. I will prepare for Myself a suit of flesh, and I shall leave my throne of glory and will become Emanuel, which being interpreted will mean God among men. And I will redeem My creation back unto Myself. For this is My divine will for man. I shall be his father and he my child. I shall be his shepherd and He my sheep. I shall be his savior and he My redeemed. Earth! Prepare thee My suit of flesh. For I shall take on the flesh of man and shall walk among them that I might reconcile man back unto me Myself.

(Music/Dance)

Lights/Curtains

ACT II

NARRATOR #1

And all things in the earth began to work together so that God's word might be fulfilled and His divine will accomplished. All things—great and small—worked together that the plan of God might be made manifest unto every created thing upon the earth.

NARRATOR #1

Now Adam knew Eve his wife, and she conceived and bore Cain, and said:

EVE

I have acquired a man from the Lord.

NARRATOR #1

And again bore his brother Abel. (Lights) And Abel was a keeper of sheep, but Cain was a tiller of the ground. And in the process of time it came to pass that Cain brought of the fruit of the ground an offering unto the Lord. And Abel brought also the firstlings of his flock. And for Abel's offering God had much respect and joy. But for Cain's offering God had neither respect nor joy. And because of this Cain become very angry and jealous.

CAIN

Cain why has God not honored my offering as He has yours? Why has He found such joy and satisfaction with your tiny offering, yet He has despised the firstlings of my flock which are greater? Is not my offering as great as yours?

ABEL

Cain, though you are my brother, I cannot speak for God. No one can. For only God knows the heart of God. Worry not, Cain, but pray and let the Father reveal these things unto you. (Abel turns to leave but Cain hurriedly picks up a large stick and strikes him across his head. Abel falls dead. Cain scrambles to hide his brother's bloody body in the brushes and to clean the blood from the earth.)

VOICE

Cain, why are thou so angry? And why hath thou countenance changed so? And where is thou brother, Abel?

CAIN

I know not where my brother is, Lord. Why ask thou me where is my brother? Am I my brother's keeper?

VOICE

What is this evil thing that thou has done unto thou brother, Cain?

CAIN

I know not what you mean, Lord.

VOICE

Your brother's blood cries out unto Me from the earth, Cain. You have committed the first murder in all the earth. Because of a jealous heart, you have killed your own brother and have lied to Me. And now thou are cursed from the earth which has opened her mouth to receive thou brother's blood from your hand. A fugitive and a vagabond shall thou be in all the earth.

CAIN

No, Lord!!! Please! My punishment is greater than I can bear.

VOICE

It will be so. Now go. (Cain turns and departs slowly.)

NARRATOR #2

Now it came to pass, when men began to multiply on the face of the earth, and daughters were born to them, that the sons of God saw the daughters of men, that they were beautiful; and they took wives for themselves of all whom they chose. And the Lord said:

VOICE

My Spirit shall not strive with man forever, for he is indeed flesh

NARRATOR #1

Then the Lord saw that the wickedness of man was great in the earth, and that every intent of the thoughts of his heart was only evil continually. And the Lord was sorry that He had made man on the earth and He was grieved in His heart. So the Lord said:

VOICE

I will destroy man whom I have created from the dust of the earth, both man and beast, creeping things and birds of the air, for I am sorry that I have made them.

NARRATOR #2

But Noah found grace in the eyes of the Lord. (Noah and family are finishing dinner. Noah finishes and goes out into the desert to pray. While in prayer God speaks to Noah.)

VOICE

The end of all flesh has come become Me, Noah; behold I will destroy all flesh with the earth for the desires of their hearts are evil and are turned far away from Me. The earth is wicked and violent. All flesh is corrupt. But you, Noah, have found grace in my eyes. Therefore, Noah, make yourself an ark of gopherwood. Make rooms in the ark, and cover it inside and outside with pitch. You will make the ark three hundred cubits in length, fifty cubits in width and thirty cubits high. And behold, I Myself am bringing floodwaters on the earth to destroy from under heaven all flesh in which is the breath of life. Everything that is on the earth shall die, except those things that are brought upon the ark for safekeeping that they may be used to replenish the earth after the flood.

NARRATOR #2

Thus Noah did. According to all God commanded him, Noah did. So Noah and his family and the animals went into the ark, and God Himself shut the door of the ark and secured it with His grace. And the waters prevailed exceedingly on the earth. And all flesh died that moved on the earth; birds and cattle and beasts and every creeping thing that creeps on the earth, and every man. All in whose nostrils was the breath of the spirit of life, all that was on the dry land died. God destroyed them all. Only Noah and those who were with him in the ark remained alive in all the earth. (Lights down. Storms and lightning can be heard. Birds and a rainbow appear on stage.) But the earth had not yet yielded a vessel worthy of providing a suit of flesh for the Messiah, and so all things great and small, continued to work together to prepare a suit of flesh for the Divine One. (Yuletide music/dance.)

LIGHTS

(Lights. Hammering and chattering can be heard in the background. Overseers voices and crackling whips can also be heard. Workers are laboring to construct the Tower of Babel.)

WORKER #1

Come, let us watch as the laborers build for us a city, and a tower whose top reaches into the heavens; lest we be scattered abroad over the face of the whole earth.

WORKER #2

When they are done we shall have made a name among names for ourselves. How great shall others says we are, and shall praise our names for generations to come as if we were gods ourselves.

WORKER #1

Excellent idea. And well said. When we are done we will have a tower whose top will reach into the heavens.

WORKER #2

And whose base will sit upon the earth. How great a name shall we have in all the lands and in all the generations to come.

VOICE

Let us go down and confound their language that they may not understand one another's speech. Indeed the people are one and they all have one language. Therefore, this thing which they have set out to do, it and nothing that they set their minds to do will be impossible for them to accomplish.

NARRATOR #1

So the Lord scattered them abroad from there over the face of all the earth, and they ceased building the city. Therefore, even today its name is called Babel because there the Lord confused the language of all the earth; and from there the Lord scattered them abroad over the face of the entire earth. Yet there was not a suit of flesh prepared in all the earth for the coming of the Divine One. God's command still remained unfulfilled.

NARRATOR #2

Now the Lord said to Abram . . .

VOICE

Get thee out of thy country, and from thy kindred and from thy father's house, unto a land that I will shew thee: And I will make of thee a great nation, and I will bless thee, and make thy name great; and thou shalt be a blessing: And I will bless them that bless thee, and curse him that curse thee: and in thee shall all families of the earth be blessed.

NARRATOR #2

And so Abram departed, as the Lord had spoken unto him. (Abraham and family exit.) And with him Abram took Lot, his nephew, Sarai, his wife, and all their substance that they had gathered, and the souls that they had gotten in Haran. Abram was seventy and five years old when he departed out of Haran.

(Abraham is alone on stage.) Now when Abram was ninety years old and nine, the Lord appeared (enters the Spirit of God. Only His back can be seen.) unto Abraham and said:

VOICE

I am the Almighty God; walk before Me, and be thou perfect. And I will make My covenant between Me and thee, and will multiply thee exceedingly.

(Abraham falls to his knees) As for Me, behold my covenant is with thee, and thou shalt be a father of many nations. Neither shall thy name any more be called Abram, but they name shall be Abraham; for a father of many nations have I made thee. And I will make thee exceedingly fruitful, and I will make nations of thee, and kings shall come out of thee. And I will establish My covenant between Me and thee and thy seed after thee in their generations for an everlasting covenant to be a God unto thee, and to thy seed after thee.

NARRATOR #2

But even yet, there was not one in all the earth worthy to birth the Messiah into the flesh. Thus the search for one such woman in all the earth continued.

(Music, laughter and frolicking abound. There is mischief everywhere. The setting is Sodom and Gomorrah. Abraham is kneeling on the opposite end of the stage.)

VOICE

Because the cry of Sodom and Gomorrah is very grievous, I will go down now and see whether the people have grown as wicked as the cries of their mouth that my heart hears continually. And if it be so, then I shall destroy the cities. (Abraham rises and starts toward Sodom and Gomorrah. As he nears the cities he frolicking becomes louder and the behavior is obviously more and more outrageous. He ponders, then pleas with God . . .)

ABRAHAM

Father, wilt thou destroy the righteous with the wicked? By chance if thou should find 50 righteous people in the city, would You not spare the wicked for the sake of the 50 righteous?

VOICE

If I find 50 righteous in the entire city of Sodom, then I will spare all the city for the sake of the 50 righteous.

ABRAHAM

(Abraham starts toward the cities again, but is overwhelmed by the frolicking and misbehavior one again. Again he ponders then asks God . . .) By chance, Father, if there be not 50 but 45. Will You spare the city then?

VOICE

My faithful servant, Abraham, by chance You should find forty and five righteous people in all the city, I will not destroy even the wicked for the sake of the 45 righteous.

ABRAHAM

(Abraham heads out again only to be totally disturbed with the evilness and lewdness prevalent in the cities.) Behold, I have not taken to bargain with You, Lord, for I am but dust and ashes, but Sodom is wicked. This we know. How be it then if there should be 40 righteous people in the city?

VOICE

I have heard your heart, Abraham. And if I should find 40 righteous people in Sodom, I will spare the entire city for the sake of the 40 righteous.

ABRAHAM

(Once again as he draws closer to the cities.) Father, forgive me as I have taken upon me to speak to the Lord. But in all of the wicked city, if thou would find 20 righteous people, would You yet spare the city?

VOICE

I will not destroy it for the sake of twenty of my people.

ABRAHAM

(Finally, Abraham offers his last request.) Let not the Lord be angry with his manservant, but I will speak just once more. In all of the city of Sodom, if 10 righteous people be found, would Thou still spare the entire city for the sake of the ten?

VOICE

I will not destroy Sodom for the sake of ten righteous people

NARRATOR

But ten righteous people were not to be found in the wicked Sodom . . . and so God sent his angels to destroy the city.

ANGEL #1

(To Lot) Hast thou here any more family members? Sons and sons-in law? Daughters and daughters-in-law?

LOT

I have.

ANGEL #2

Whatever thou hast in this city, you must gather it up and leave immediately. For we will destroy this place, because the cry of them is waxen great before the face of the Lord; and the Lord hath sent us to destroy it.

ANGEL #1

You must hasten your escape, Lot. For we will not destroy this city until you and your family have escaped out of it. Leave thou now quickly, Lot, and get your family high into the hills.

ANGEL #2

And look not behind you as you escape. For surely if you should look back upon this iniquity, you shall also be consumed.

LOT

I have heard your instructions and I and my family will heed your words.

ANGEL #1

You and your family must go now, Lot. Go.

ANGEL #2

Hurry! And remember, Lot, DO NOT LOOK BACK. DO NOT LOOK BACK!! (In the background, the cities are being destroyed.)

NARRATOR

But his wife disobeyed. She looked back and was turned into a pillar of salt. Even now, there was no woman of virtue suited to birth the Messiah into the flesh. And thus the search continued.

NARRATOR #1

Abraham and Sarah, but not one worthy of giving birth to the Messiah.
Rebekah and Isaac, but not one worthy of giving birth to the Messiah.
Rachel and Jacob, but not one worthy of giving birth to the Messiah.
Yet the earth continued to prepare a suit of flesh for the coming of the Messiah.

NARRATOR #2

Now Moses kept the flock of Jethro his father in law, the priest of Midian: and he led the flock to the backside of the desert, and came to the mountain of God even to Horeb. And the angel of the Lord appeared unto Moses in a flame of fire out of the midst of a bush: and he looked, and, behold, the bush burned with fire, and the bush was not consumed. And Moses said:

MOSES

I will now turn aside, and see this great sight, why the bush is not burnt.

VOICE

Moses. Moses.

MOSES

Here am I.

VOICE

Draw not nigh hither; put off thy shoes from thy feet for the place where upon thou standest is Holy ground. I am the God of thy father, the God of Abraham, the God of Jacob and the God of Issac. (Abraham hides his face.) I have surely seen the affliction of my people which are in Egypt, and have heard their cry by reason of their taskmasters; for I know their sorrows; and I am come down to deliver them out of the land of the Egyptians, and to bring them up out of that land unto a good land and a large, unto a land overflowing with milk and honey. Come now therefore, and I will send thee unto Pharoah, that thou mayest bring forth my people the children of Israel out of Egypt.

MOSES

Who am I, Lord, that I should go unto Pharoah and bring forth the children of Israel out of Egypt? Behold, when I come unto the children of Israel, and say unto them, The God of your fathers hath sent me unto you; and they shall say to me, What is his name? What shall I say unto them?

VOICE

You shall say unto them, His name is I AM THAT I AM. Thou shalt say unto the children of Israel I AM hath sent me unto you. And I am sure that the King of Egypt will not let you go, no not by a mighty hand, but I will stretch out my hand and smite Egypt with all my wonders which I will do in the midst thereof; and after that he will let you go. (Moses exits then returns leading the children of Israel. They arrive at the Red Sea when suddenly . . .)

MAN #1

My God, Moses!!! Are you a fool man? Why you have lead out of Egypt right into the Red Sea? What kind of Promised land is that?

WOMAN #1

Moses! How could you do such an evil thing to us?

MAN #2

She is right, Moses. We have the Red Sea at our front and Pharaoh's angry army to our backs. What do we do now?

MAN #3

We were much better off to have stayed in bondage than to follow the like of you Moses. I knew you would get us all killed.

WOMAN #3

Why he's nothing more than a blundering idiot who will get us all killed. Pharaoh's army is quickly advancing upon us and the waters of the Red Sea stand ready to swallow us like fish and all you can do is to stand there and stare into the heavens?

MAN #4

Kill him! Kill him! Kill Moses and return to the bondage of Egypt.

CROWD

(Advancing toward Moses) Kill him! Kill him!

MOSES

(Turning to face the crowd.) You man. (pointing to Man 4) How have you eaten in this desert since your liberation from Pharaoh? And you woman! You were sickly in Egypt and yet you have been without as much as a cough during our sojourn through this wilderness. How so? Which one of you hath seen sickness for one day or starvation for one meal? Which one of you hath had death visited upon your family? Which one of you hath not seen the presence of the Almighty by a pillar of smoke during the night and a cloud during the day? When did the God of our fathers ever leave or forsake us? Did He not say that He would deliver you from the bondage of Pharaoh? Then will He not do just what He has promised? Stand still and behold the powers of the great I AM. (Turns and raises his staff) Oh, Great Jehovah, you have guided our footsteps to this place at this time that You might show yourself to be the great I AM THAT I AM. Now we lift up our faith in the presence of adversity and certain defeat, yet we claim victory because we know our strength in You. And so, we shall stand firm in the presence of danger and death and say to you the GREAT I AM, be thou our Almighty God even in the midst of these adversities!

MAN #2

LOOK! LOOK! Can this thing be?

LADY #1

The Red Sea is parting. How can it be?

MAN 4

The floor of the sea is as dry as the dessert.

MAN 1

It's a miracle! It's a miracle.

WOMAN 3

Truly, Moses, you are a man of the Most High God.

MOSES

God's own hands for our safe crossing have built a passage of water. Now we must hurry before the army catches us to us. (Many positive speeches are heard during the passage.)

PERSON 1

What a leader this Moses is. Truly he must be of God.

PERSON 2

Moses is a sent leader. I am glad God has sent him to lead us out of Egypt.

PERSON 3

He is truly blessed of the Lord. Long live Moses.

CROWD

Long live Moses! Long live Moses!

NARRATOR #1

Yet there was not one fit to birth the Messiah into the flesh. (Lights) The judges and the kings. Samuel and Saul. David and Joshua. Jonathan and Daniel. Joshua and Ezekiel. Solomon, Daniel, and Jeremiah. Benjamin and Joseph. Great men of statue and renown, yet out of their loins combined came not one woman seen fit by God to be his earthly mother. And so, the search continued.

NARRATOR #2

And all things in the earth began to work together that God's word might be fulfilled and His will accomplished. All things—great and small—worked together that the plan of God might be made manifest unto every creation in the earth.

ABRAM

I have been in prayer and meditation with the father, Sari. And God has spoken unto me and has said that He has blessed your womb with a child. You, Sari, shall give birth to our baby.

SARI

(Laughing) Abram! What foolishness you speak! Have you not forgotten your own age? And that my womb is no more fruitful? Surely you have lied on your God.

ABRAM

As God has spoken it, Sari, by the power of His word, it shall come to pass.

NARRATOR

And they were blessed with a son called Isaac. And Abraham loved Isaac with all his heart for he knew he was a gift from the Lord. And so he taught and prayed with Isaac much as the boy grew.

VOICE

Abraham!

ABRAHAM

Here am I, Lord.

VOICE

Take your son, your only son, Isaac, whom you love, and go to the region of Moriah. There you will offer him up as a sacrifice upon a burnt offering on one of the mountains there.

NARRATOR #1

And though he Abraham loved Isaac dearly, he yet obeyed the word of God. Abraham arrived at the foot of the mountain with Isaac and a servant and prepared himself to carry out God's command to him.

ABRAHAM

(To the servant) Stay here while the boy and I go over there to worship the Lord. After we have worshipped we will return back here to you.

ISAAC

Father?

ABRAHAM

Yes, my son.

ISAAC

I see that the fire and the wood are here, but where is the lamb to be offered up as the burnt offering?

ABRAHAM

The Lord Himself will supply us a lamb, my son. The Lord will do this. I am sure. (Abraham binds his son and lays him on the offering table, then prepares to sacrifice him.)

VOICE

Abraham! Abraham!

ABRAHAM

Here am I, Lord.

VOICE

Lay not a hand upon the boy. Your obedience has been witnessed by God Himself. In your faith is the Father well pleased and He has accounted it to you as righteousness before him. The creations know that you fear God because you have not withheld from him your son, even your only son.

And God Himself hath sworn by Himself that since this day you have not withheld even your only son, that He will bless you and make your descendents as numerous as the stars in the sky and as the sand on the seashore. (The sound of a lamb can be heard. Abraham unbinds the boy and goes over to the thicket to remove the ram that is caught there. He returns with the lamb and places it on the burnt offering table. There he sacrifices it.)

ABRAHAM

Now we will return to the servant at the foot of the mountain.

NARRATOR

Yet . . . there was not a suit of flesh prepared to receive the Messiah into the earth. And so the search continued. Prophecy after prophecy. Miracle after miracle. Revelation after revelation. The process of preparing a suit of flesh for the coming of the Messiah continued.

ISAIAH

Nevertheless there shall be no more gloom for those who were in distress. In the past, he humbled the land of Zebulun and the land of Naphtali, but in the future he will honor Galilee of the Gentiles, by the way of the sea, along the Jordan—

The people walking in darkness have seen a great light; on those living in the land of the shadow of death a light has dawned.

You have enlarged the nation and increased their joy; they rejoice before you as people rejoice at the harvest as men rejoice when dividing the plunder.

For as in the day of Midian's defeat, you have shattered the yoke that burdens them, the bar across their shoulders, the rod of their oppressor.

Every warrior's boot used in battle and every garment rolled in blood will be destined for burning, will be fuel for the fire.

For unto us a child is born, unto us a son is given, and the government will be on his shoulders. And he will be called Wonder Counselor, mighty god, Everlasting Father, Prince of Peace.

Of the increase of his government and peace there will be no end. He will reign on David's throne and over his kingdom, establishing and upholding it with justice and righteousness from that time on and forever.

The zeal of the Lord Almighty will accomplish this.

NARRATOR

Yet there was not one fit to birth the Messiah into the flesh. (Lights) The judges and the kings. Samuel and Saul. David and Joshua. Jonathan and Daniel. Jeremiah and Ezekiel. Solomon and Ruth. Boaz and Naomi. Benjamin and Rebekah. Joseph and Beersheba. Great men and women of renown and Biblical statue, yet out of their loins and wombs combined came not one offspring seen fit by God to be His earthly mother. And then . . . .

(Stage is amuck with sinners feasting in the lusts of the flesh. Dancing, partying, drinking, and frolicking are everywhere)

VOICE

Surely there must be one righteous among them. Just one. Just one who has sanctified her mind, preserved her soul, and committed her will to serve me— to me and me alone her God. Surely there must be just one . . . just one among them. (Enters Mary. Crosses downstage of the heathens. Kneels and worships.) There! Proned before my throne and in reverence to me is she by whom and through whom I shall deliver a savior which shall be my word wrapped in flesh and shall be known as the son of man. He shall be great. He shall be mighty. He shall be all powerful. He shall be king of kings. Lord of Lords. The mighty counselor. The prince of peace. He shall be Immanuel—which translated shall mean God with man

YES! YES1 I-even I God-shall make myself flesh and blood and dwell among men. I shall be their savior. I shall be their Lord. And I shall deliver them from the evil one. I shall destroy their yokes and remove their burdens. Yes, yes! Even I God shall take on a suit of flesh and dwell among men that they who shall receive me shall likewise dwell in my kingdom as heirs. And I shall be called Jesus the Christ. For I will be the anointed one. The appointed one. The divine one. Who shall save them from their sins, deliver them from the hands of the great deceiver, and redeem them back unto myself. Yes, yes! The

Christ. The Christ. I shall be the Christ among men. I shall be Jesus the Christ. (Music/Dance. Lights.)

GUY #1

(Spotting Mary as she prays and making fun of her to his peers who have been engaging in frivolities with him.) The woman there! Who might she be?

GIRL #1

She is called Mary. She is the (gesturing) wife to be of Joseph—the carpenter (Laughing).

GUY #2

Carpenter? (Hearty laughter) Woman! Woman! I say, how is it that your father has betrothed you to a (snickering)—carpenter? (laughter).

GUY #1

And why is it you have not bothered to join our festivities this evening? Are you Mary as I have been told about you?

MARY

What you have heard is true. My name is Mary. I have chosen not to partake in your festivities as they fail to glorify my God. I am sanctified for His purpose and use and am not my own.

GIRL #2

Could you not look upon her countenance and expect that this woman would speak such?

MARY

Why hath thou spoken such a thing against me? In time past, have I wronged thee? Injured thee? Forsaken thee? Why speaketh thou then so sharply against my innocence?

GIRL #1

(Flirting with Guy #1 as she speaks) She has spoken such because she fears your heart to be less pure than your words.

MARY

Should not my father in heaven be the judge of that?

GUY #2

Yes! Yes! How excellent an idea.

GIRL #1

Excellent?

GUY #2

Excellent, as I have spoken. For how can we judge one another unless we ourselves are righteous enough to do so without error?

GUY #1

Let her God then be her judge. And may He proclaim her righteousness.

GIRL #2

Yes! By bringing forth a miracle to all mankind through her.

GIRL #1

Yes, then we will know that she is indeed a righteous woman in the eyes of her own God.

GUY #2

That God would look down from his throne and produce a miracle to all mankind through the likes of a betrothed carpenter's wife is but a witty thought. Come for we have tarried here too long with the betrothed carpenter's wife. Let us make our way to Bethlehem. For there surely we shall find much wine and merriment . . . and fewer carpenters' wives. (Mocking her as they exit).

MARY

(Softly and forgivingly to the departed group) May God be with you all. (Resumes her prayer. Finishes. Exit. Lights.)

NARRATOR

Now in those days Caesar Augustus issued a decree that a census should be taken of the entire Roman world. And everyone went to his own town to register. So Joseph also went up from the town of Nazareth in Galilee to Judea, to Bethlehem the town of David, because he belonged to the house and the line of David. He went there to register with Mary who was pledged to be married to him and was expecting a child. While they were there, the time came for the baby to be born.

MARY

Not a single room in all the city, Joseph?

JOSEPH

None in all of the city, my lady. Every inn is filled with travelers who have come here to pay their taxes. We will just have to find ourselves a place where you can be comfortable. Me? I can sleep any place. Wait here, Mary. I will go yonder and inquire of the innkeeper if he has one room remaining. I will be but a minute. (Exits. Returns momentarily, but less gleefully.)

MARY

(With good humor) I have heard his reply by merely listening to your countenance. There are no more rooms.

JOSEPH

You are a wonderfully smart woman, Mary. But that is not all that the innkeeper said however.

MARY

No? Did he point you to a room then?

JOSEPH

Not a room. There are no rooms to be had in the entire city. But the innkeeper has granted us permission to sleep in the stable behind the inn . . . if we would like. There he said we could stay for free and far as long as we might have to.

(Agreeably) Why then do we tarry here man? On, I say, to the stable!! (Laughter. The couple arrives at the stable and enters. Joseph assists Mary in becoming as comfortable as possible then begins tidying up the area.)

MARY

Joseph?

JOSEPH

Yes, my dear.

MARY

Have I vexed you and angered your spirit toward me?

JOSEPH

(Surprised) Mary? Why such a question? You yourself are sure that such could never happen.

MARY

I do hope not. Yet I know that the child that is within me is not of your loins. Yet you suffer all of this for me.

JOSEPH

As I have said to you, Mary. I was visited by God's own angels and told that you were with child, and that the child within your belly was that which was placed there by the Holy Ghost. Of this I am persuaded and cannot doubt.

That child which is within you is not of flesh and blood . . . but of the Spirit. You, Mary, are blessed among all the women of the earth.

MARY

And you have said that because?

JOSEPH

Because it is true, Mary. How many other women are upon the entire earth?

MARY

Many Joseph.

JOSEPH

And of them all, Mary, (Mary is silently reacting to labor contraction pains. Joseph is not aware as he is working as he talks to her) whom did God Himself choose as the human vessel through which he would enter into the earth?

MARY

Me, Joseph. J-J-Joseph.

JOSEPH

You are correct, Mary. And you are blessed among all women upon the earth. You, Mary have found special favor in the eyes and heart of God the almighty. What a pleasant savor you must be in His nostril.

MARY

I am but His servant. He is free to use me as He wills. J-J-Jos . . . .

JOSEPH

I am also blessed of the Lord, Mary.

MARY

Jo-Jo-Jo . . . .

JOSEPH

For to have been visited and warned by the angels about your pregnancy is a wonderful experience that only the spouse of the woman who will give birth to the Messiah can experience. That too is a miracle for me.

MARY

Jo . . . Jo . . . Joseph

JOSEPH

(Skyward) The sky is so beautiful tonight. It is divinely beautiful. It is as if if you looked hard enough you could actually see the eyes of God staring back at you.

MARY

(Highly discomforted) Joseph! Joseph!

JOSEPH

(Still looking skyward) It's as if Jehovah Himself is watching over the earth to ensure that His own will is done this night. (Notices Mary's discomfort and races to her side.) Mary!! Why did you not say something to me?

MARY

(Sarcastically) Joseph . . .

JOSEPH

Mary, I believe now is the appointed time for the coming of the Messiah.

MARY

Ah-h-h-h-h! Ah-h-h-h-h! Joseph! I do agree with you.

JOSEPH

The Messiah. The Messiah.

MARY

Joseph. God is disrobing Himself of his divinity . . . of His power . . . of His glory and is preparing to step out of the spirit and into the flesh. He is about to step out of timelessness and into time. Ah-h-h-h-h.

JOSEPH

He's stepping Mary. Down through time. Down out of eternity and into the now. He's stepping down from his throne to our earth. He's stepping . . . (angels, wise men, cattles, kings bearing gifts all are entering and assembly round the manger) He's stepping. Out of the past . . . out of His perfection . . . out of His glory . . . out of his exalted status . . . God is stepping. (The mighty men of old enter, though they appear as spirits, and observe the birth of the Messiah.)

MARY

And into the flesh shall He step and become as one of us, Joseph. He shall become a man and shall be called Emanuel.

JOSEPH

Which when translated means God among man.

MARY

And He will walk as one of us . . . and talk as one of us . . . . and experience life as one of us . . . and live and even die as one of us. But He will be more than just one of us. He will be God among us. He will teach us . . . and lead us . . . . and inspire us . . . and deliver us . . . . and save us . . . and redeem us . . . back unto Himself.

JOSEPH

Is it yet time, Mary? (Rubbing Mary's stomach)

MARY

The time is nigh, Joseph as I can feel the Messiah taking on flesh and form in my belly as we speak.

JOSEPH

And out of your belly, Mary . . .

MARY

No, Joseph. Out of heaven. Out of heaven Ah-h-h-h! Joseph the hour is now. Let us pray that we have done all that we have been commanded by the Lord.

JOSEPH

Yes, Mary. I feel that we are surrounded by great friends of the faith who have been allowed to return to the earth realm to see their God take on His suit of flesh. Out of our spirits let us touch and agree and pray as the Messiah enters into the flesh. (Music/Song/Dance.)

JOSEPH

Mary! Mary! You have done it!

MARY

I am but His handmaiden, Joseph. Be it unto me as God hath seen fit. But of myself I have done nothing more than you. God hath fixed all these matters.

JOSEPH

Emmanuel. The promised child. The son who was given. The shepherd of the lost sheep. The Messiah and savior of the world. He's here. He's here. And he has entered the earth through the womb of a virgin—and a carpenter's wife. How mighty is our Lord. (Angels are descending and singing "Glory to God In The Highest." A savior. A redeemer. A messiah. (Holding the baby aloft and presenting him to both the heavens and the audience Joseph announces . . .) As promised by creator, opposed by the evil one, and now manifested in the flesh . . . BEHOLD EMMANUEL! BEHOLD EMMANUEL! GOD AMONG MAN!! (Finale. Lights)

CURTAINS

I Want to
Dance with
My Angels

Cast of Characters

Father (Reggie)

Mother (Grace)

Daughter (Becky)

Doctor (Dr. Scott)

Nurse 1 (Nurse Grace)

Nurse 2 (Nurse Holbet)

Arnie

Blackhawk

Ginnie

Frankie

Medical Attendant

ACT I

SCENE I

(Mother enters attired in common clothes. The living room of the family's house has not been cleaned despite her earlier instructions to her daughter. She carefully observes the house as she crosses to the closet area, relieves herself of her coat and hat, turns off the blarring t.v. then calls to her daughter whom she presumes is off stage . . .)

GRACE:

Rebecca! (Pause but no answer) Rebecca! (Pause but no answer. Goes over and looks in bedroom area.) BECKY-Y-Y! OH-H-H BECKY!! You in there girl? If you are, you need to beat feet out here right now girl . . . and quick too! Me and you got something we need to discuss—RIGHT NOW!! BECKY!!! (No answer. She now realizes Becky is not at home. Talking indiscriminately to herself.) Lord, I tell you the truth. If I didn't love you and weren't committed to giving you TOTAL control over me, my thoughts, my ways (mindfully) and my tongue—You know I would have some mighty choice words for that child right about now. BECKY!!! Look like the more I tell that child to go left she just proves to me just how determined she is to go right. Every time I tell her to stand still—Lord, it just seems to me like she just got to move just a little bit more. Everything I say don't—she do. I say no—she say yes. I say go—she says stay. I say okay then let's stay—what does she do? She grabs her coat and gets ready to go. Lord, I just don't know. (She's so busy cleaning and fussing that she has not seen her husband enter L) What else can I do? Her father and I have held her up before you in prayer all her life. Even while I was carrying her in this very belly. We've taken her to church every Sunday. We've taught

51

her well and provided and disciplined her as Your word has commanded us to do . . . so now, Lord, tell me . . . please, Lord . . . PLEASE . . . tell me . . . what else can we do with this child? It just seems like nothing we do is enough. Nothing we know is good or smart enough. Nothing we teach her is "cool" enough. Now I just want to know, Lord, what else can we do?

REGGIE:

(Without speaking goes over and touches his wife on her shoulder. She is startled.) Well, I don't usually go around trying to answer prayers for the master, but as your husband, I would say that for starters you can welcome your other half home from a hard day's work. Then you can tell me what's that smelling so good in here.

GRACE:

Oh! Hi Honey! (Goes over and hugs him) Sorry you caught me having another one of my one-sided talks with the Lord.

REGGIE:

One sided?

GRACE:

Yeah. That is I seem to be doing all the talking by myself. I'm just HOPING he's doing all the listening and answering though. (Quickly turning reflective and pensive) For the last couple of years it seems like that's all I do *IS* have one-sided talks with the Lord about that same old hardheaded child. And I know He hears me—every time we have one of these talks—but it's like He never seems to answer my question.

REGGIE:

And just what question is that, Honey? Maybe I can answer it for you. (Sitting down and putting his feet up on the table.)

GRACE:

(Quickly removing his feet from the table) No Sweetheart. I don't think so. I mean I know you want to, but this is an answer I need to hear from God. (Laughingly) Just to be sure. 'Cause this is one answer I NEED to be sure is STRAIGHT from the Lord Himself.

REGGIE:

That bad, huh?

GRACE:

That bad, Honey. That bad. I mean, Reggie, sometimes, it's just like that child isn't even ours. I mean—(struggling) it's as if she didn't even come out of me at all. It's like she never grew up in a good Christian home—or knew the Lord—or had any church upbringing—or even fears God's commandments at all. Reggie? (very seriously)

REGGIE:

Yeah Baby.

GRACE:

What happens to a fetus before it becomes a baby?

REGGIE:

(Looking at her over the paper he's now reading.) WH-H-HAT?

GRACE:

You know. T-T-The Bible says whom God has called he has predestined before birth. And that he has sanctified them for his purpose and has even sealed them with his grace.

REGGIE:

Yeah? And so?

GRACE:

So-o-o-o (Trying to make him understand her point. Using hand gesture to assist) what happens to those who are not called by God? Are they just here? Do they serve a purpose? Were they predestined by (making quotes with her fingers) some other power too? Before their birth?

REGGIE:

Honey! Honey! Honey! Listen. Just listen at you!! I know the child didn't wash the dishes . . . and she probably didn't clean her room either . . . nor take out the trash like you asked her . . . but, BABY, that doesn't mean that the child is a demon. It just means that she's probably just behaving normally.

GRACE:

Normally?!

REGGIE:

Normally. Now come on, Honey, you don't really believe Rebecca is the only child in town who has to be told more than once to pick up after herself . . . or to clean her room . . . or to wash the dishes. Do you? Do you really believe that? That she's the ONLY teenager in this whole city who has to be told to do something as undesirable as clean up behind herself twice?

GRACE:

Reggie, this is not just behind herself. This is BESIDE herself. IN FRONT of herself. ABOVE herself. BENEATH herself. Honey, listen. I'm not suggesting that it was the devil that got a hold of that child while she was still forming inside of me.

REGGIE:

Oh no? Then just what ARE you suggesting?

GRACE:

I'm saying . . . well . . . maybe . . . I don't know. I just thought maybe it was little dusty and cluttered inside there (pointing to her stomach) when she was forming and . . . well . . . you know . . . maybe she just kind of got use to a junky and dusty environment . . . and now we just can't get her out of the habit. (Disgusted) Shoot! I don't know. I guess that is why I was praying about it when you came in.

REGGIE:

(Laughing) Does that very unreal—can't be true—totally silly sounding excuse satisfy you? Does it make you happy and stop you from fussing and complaining to both me and the Lord?

GRACE:

Complaining to the Lord? Who? I wasn't complaining to the Lord. Not me. I sure wasn't.

REGGIE:

Then who was that you were complaining to when I came in the door a few minutes ago?

GRACE:

Nobody. I was just asking the Lord to show me what to do. But I wasn't complaining to anybody. (Laughter) And by the way . . . you wanted to know what was smelling so good in here? (She's now sitting on the couch next to him)

REGGIE:

I did when I first came in.

GRACE:

But you don't now?

REGGIE:

I already do. (Sniffs her neck) And whatever it's called you sure do make it smell even better.

GRACE:

(In a flirtatious manner) Why thank you, Baby.

REGGIE:

Listen. I know you're tired and I could use a little relief tonight myself, so guess what.

GRACE:

I give up. What?

REGGIE:

I want you to go over there, get your coat, put it on, and come and join me for a most delicious meal at the restaurant of your choice.

GRACE:

(Moving hurriedly) Well, boy, don't ask me twice. Come to think about it, I heard that new soul food restaurant just off Spruce Street is great!

REGGIE:

(Getting up but is met quickly by his wife who hastily assists him with his hat and coat) Soul food? I thought you were depressed just a second ago AND on a diet. Besides that I was thinking more along the lines of soup and a salad.

GRACE:

Hey! Hey! Hey! Didn't you just say the restaurant of my choice, or did I misunderstand you?

REGGIE:

S-sure I did, I said the restaurant of your choice, but I didn't know.

GRACE:

Alright then. Soup and salad ain't my choice tonight, baby. (Pulling him to the door.) My choice tonight is some good old fashioned collard greens that taste so good they make you want to jump up and slap somebody—ANYBODY. Child the kind that make your toes spread when you eat'em. Then a few candid yams and some macaroni and cheese with a half a slab of ribs . . . o-o-o-oh Lordy have mercy! And child don't let me forget about a side order of potato salad that tastes so good you'd swear your mama must've made it herself.

REGGIE:

B-b-baby what about your diet?

GRACE:

Not now, Reggie. I'm too busy trying to do what the Word of God says do, Sweetie.

REGGIE:

The Word of God?

GRACE:

Yeah. I'm trying to call those things that are not so that by the time I get to the restaurant they *will* be. See what I mean? Let me see now, I'm gonna have some sweet ice tea to drink, so now what do I want for desert?

REGGIE:

(Exiting. Lights dying.) DESERT? Lord have mercy! (Black. Music.)

ACT I

SCENE II

(Daughter and friends are hanging out on a street corner on the rough side of town.)

BECKY:

Come on baby. Come on baby. Come on baby. Let me see what you got. Let me see what you got. Let me see what you got (Blowing on the dice, then rolling) for Big Bad Becky!! Ah-h-h-h YEAH baby! JOY TO THE WORLD.

ARNOLD:

(The quiet and "different" member of the group. He's always making corrections when they other youths "step out of line.")

Chill out over there with that, Becky. I heard that. What you think you doing, girl?

BECKY:

(To Arnold) What up with you, man? Say? What's the matter little Arnie, the cat's got your tongue? Meow! Meow!

ARNOLD:

Naw. I'm just saying man. You need to chill out with the joy to the world and talking to the dice and all man. See what uh'm saying? How come you

59

can't just roll the bones like everybody else instead of trying to get all intimate with'em and kissing'em n' stuff? I mean, talking just for me myself, I just don't like it when you go round talkin' bout some joy to the world and all, dog. That's all I'm trying saying, man.

BLACKHAWK:

What up man? You gone religious . . . sanctified . . . or something on me dawg? Know what um' saying? I mean like why you hatin' on the sister just for saying "Joy to the world" and stuff dawg?

ARNOLD:

I wasn't hatin' on her, Blackhawk. I was just suggesting to her to be a little more careful about the words she uses to express her feelings and thoughts.

BLACKHAWK:

(Grabbing Arnold in his collar.) Boy you crazy or something? These da streets Negro! (Becoming very emotional) And out here we can say anything we want to say. Why you think we out here anyway? 'Cause we can't say what we want at home. Now here you come—little Mr. Gospel Boy—preaching that same old nonsense to us our parents been trying to drive in our heads all our lives. We don't wanna hear that mess man! If we wanted to hear that kind of junk we'd just stayed home and not been out here on night like this. If that's all you got to talk about maybe you need to get to stepping too—Mama's boy! Shoot! Don't nobody want to hear dat noise.

FRANKIE:

Now that's a word fo' yo behind, boy. Don't you ever come out here on these streets acting and thinking you in a Sunday school class or something. 'Cause if you do you show nuff gone get yanked, spanked, and made to walk the plank before church is out. (To Blackhawk) But yo,' ease up on him some,

Blackhawk. He's cool. That's just the way he is, man. Arnold's always about doing the right thing even when we're dead set on doing wrong, man. You know that, dawg. All us done tried to school that fool 'bout talking all the time like he think we sisters and decons and stuff. Mama's little boy been that way every since we met him three weeks ago.

BLACKHAWK:

That's what I'm saying man. Brother always coming out here acting like . . . shoot, I don't know! But if you ask me, he sho' don't act enough like us to BE one of us. See what I'm saying?

GINNIE:

Let it ride, man. It ain't no thang. (Notices Hawk's insistent stare.) Come on, Hawk, man! Lighten up now. What's up with you? All my man said was something about joy to world . . . or something like that, . . . And you done gone off like somebody done stole your best Sunday go to meeting suit. What's up with that, man? See what um' saying? Why all the drama over something so simple?

BLACKHAWK:

Naw. Naw that ain't it man. Y'all just can't get with this; that's all.

GINNIE:

Get with what, Hawk?

BLACKHAWK:

Y'all just can't see what I'm talking about. It's something else 'bout that brother I don't like man. I don't know what it is yet. I can't put my finger on it right now either. But it's something about you that just don't set right with

61

me. And if it's the last thing I ever do on this earth . . . um' gonna find out just what it is. And you can put your life on that.

ARNOLD:

I know. But don't worry 'bout it, Hawk, 'cause if it's the last thing in the world you do, you WILL find out what it is. I promise.

BLACKHAWK:

Yo! What's that suppose to mean? Huh? Huh? See what I'm saying? I'm trying to let it go but no-o-o this little boy just gotta keep the heat on, huh. (Approaching Arnold as he speaks.)

BECKY:

(Restraining B'Hawk) Come on now, Hawk! Chill out, man! It ain't gotta be like that—busted up knees, nose, and elbows. Just chill, man! Come on now. Chill baby.

ARNOLD:

Don't be nervous, Becky. I'll be okay.

GINNIE:

OKAY?!! OKAY?!! (Trying to restrain Blackhawk) Boy have you lost your mind or something? No, Hawk! Naw man! Come on, Hawk! Ain't no need in that! Come on now!

ARNOLD:

(Extremely calm and undisturbed) It'll be alright if you let go of Hawk. Trust me; nothing will happen to me. And I promise not to hurt him either.

GINNIE:

YOU?!! Hurt him?!! That's the least of our worries. Go on, Arnold. Get out of here. Go! Now! I can't hold Hawk back much longer!

BECKY:

You heard her! Get on out of here! All you've done every since you joined our gang was to get this kind of reaction out of him.

ARNOLD:

But what have I done to him?

BECKY:

Hey, little perfect and peaceful boy!! You listen to me and you listen to me real good. These are my friends, and any time you turn on one of us, you may as well say you've turned on all of us.

ARNOLD:

Which of your friends have I turned on, Becky? (Becky give Arnold a hard slap to the face.)

BECKY:

I said GET, Arnold. And I mean right now before we all jump you and beat you to a pulp. Now can you understand that you little Holy boy? Now you GET! (Arnold says nothing. He feels his face, drops his head, turns and exits.) You alright, dawg?

BLACKHAWK:

(Regaining his composure) Um straight. Everything's good. Um alright. (They all look at him for a moment.) I'm straight. I'm straight. Shoot! Like I said (reaches inside his shirt and retrieves a pentagram necklace) there's just something about that boy I just can't stand, but I just can't seem to put my hands on just what it is. I ain't worried about it though, I know it'll come to me sooner or later. Hey, dawg, who got the stuff y'all?

BECKY:

Who you think? ME. (Retrieves a marijuana joint from her pocket.) Fire, baby, fire, fire, fire. (Lights up the joint.) Yeah. This is just what the sister needs by the time she finishes dealing with a clown like that boy.

BLACKHAWK:

(Taking the joint from her hand and puffing on it) Aw-w man! Y'all just need to smoke home boy away! See what um' saying. He ain't even got no business being in the conversation no mo' t'night. So just forget him! He ain't nobody no how. (Puffs) Ask me that boy ain't nothing but a stone weird-o anyhow.

GINNIE:

Yeah. I admit old Arnold is about two French fries short of a happy meal.

BLACKHAWK:

Hmm! Say what you want to, but that boy is about two French fries short of any kind of meal. (Laughter)

GINNIE:

Aw-w-w-w man. (Looking at her watch) Aw-w-w shoot!

BECKY:

Whazzup, girl? You over there flipping all out and stuff! What done got into you? I know that one joint ain't jonesing you THAT hard. (Ginnie does not say anything, just shows Becky the time.) ELEVEN FIFTEEN!!! Oh, man, I'm just as good as dead!

GINNIE:

YOU? Whadda ya think about me?

BECKY:

Child that's just it. (rising as she speaks) I ain't got time to think about you. Right now I'm TOO busy thinking about myself. Lord have mercy. I ain't got no kind of idea what kind of lie I'm gonna tell my parents when I get home . . . but whatever it is I'm sure going to have to think it up on my why home. 'Cause the later I get in the bigger and better my lie gonna have to be. I'm outta here, y'all. See y'all when I see ya.

GINNIE:

Wait for me, Becky!

BECKY:

Girl don't play crazy now. You heard me say I was already going to be in big enough trouble when I get home as it is. Now you asking me to wait so I can get home later and get in even more trouble. (She is talking back over her shoulder as she heads to the exit.) I don't hardly think so, Miss Ginnie. If you plan on walking with the sister, you might need to be stepping this way—and quickly—right about now. (Can be heard practicing her explanation to her parents as they exits the stage. The boys remain on the stage smoking the joint and playing dice. LIGHTS.)

ACT I

SCENE III

REGGIE:

(They are re-entering the house. They are in a jovial mood and are laughing and singing gospel songs.) Whew-w-w!!! (Laughter) Now see that's why you have to cook so much.

GRACE:

And why is that?

REGGIE:

Girl 'cause when I take you out to eat . . . with your appetite . . . you make folks think we done over charged our EBT card and ain't got no food left up in this house.

GRACE:

Baby?

REGGIE:

Yeah?

GRACE:

We don't have an EBT card, Baby.

REGGIE:

We don't. Oh-h-h. Well shucks then! No wonder we never have any food in this house. (Laughter) Whew. I got to tell the truth, though. That Skipper's Restaurant just can't be beat on a night like this one.

GRACE:

(Becoming serious and observing the house is the same as before their departure.) Yeah. Yeah. You're right. You're absolutely right, baby.

REGGIE:

Something wrong, honey?

GRACE:

You bet'cha. (Glances at her watch) It's twelve fifteen and she's not here yet.

REGGIE:

Oh sure she's here. Even though we're late getting back, Becky knows we don't allow her to stay out past 10:00 during the week and 11:30 on weekends and holidays.

GRACE:

(Becoming very excited) Don't quote the rules to me, Reggie!! I know every single one of her rules. But that doesn't mean that she's here.

GRACE:

Baby . . . .

GRACE:

Call her, Reggie.

REGGIE:

What?

GRACE:

Call her, Reggie. CALL HER! Do just like the Lord did you and me before we were even in our mothers' wombs—CALL . . . HER . . . BY . . . HER . . . NAME!! CALL HER, REGGIE. CALL HER!

REGGIE:

GRACE!! Stop this nonsense! Quit it! Just quit it!

GRACE:

NO! Not until you call your daughter out here, Reggie. Not until I see her come from behind that door and bring her little narrow behind out here and face the music!

REGGIE:

Music! What the devil music you talking about, Grace?

GRACE:

My music, Reginald. That's what music! Mine!

REGGIE:

AH! So that's it, huh? HUH?

GRACE:

What's it, Reggie? What's it?

REGGIE:

Your music? That it, huh? You're still mad with the poor child because she didn't clean up earlier tonight like you told her to, huh? So now that you've pigged out and cleaned everything off your trough, now you want to come home and rain havoc on the child before you got to wallow in the comfort of your king size sty.

GRACE:

Yo-u-uu . . .

REGGIE:

You what? What am I now, Grace? Huh? What am I this time? A liar? Naive perhaps. A fool. (She cuts her eyes and emits an agreeable countenance.) A fool?

GRACE:

Well . . . let's just say I'm not the one that tried those shoes on, but since you did and they seem to fit so well, I wouldn't bother taking them off if I were you.

REGGIE:

I've had about all of this mess I can take for one evening. (Goes over near her door) BECKY! BECKY! Becky I hate to wake you up this time of night dear . . .

GRACE:

Liar.

REGGIE:

But I need you to come out here and let your mommy see daddy's little angel in her sleeping gown . . .

GRACE:

Naive.

REGGIE:

Then you can go straight back to bed, Angel Pooh . . .

GRACE:

Fool.

REGGIE:

Becky! Becky! BECKY! (Opens the door and peeps in. Notices she is not there. Closes the door softly and looks confusingly at wife.) She's not in there.

GRACE:

Liar.

REGGIE:

Ah! How stupid of me! Becky's in our room. Of course, she missed us while we were out. (Goes over near the door.) BECKY. BECKY. (Looks inside. Same results as before) Not there either.

GRACE:

Naive.

REGGIE:

(Standing center stage looking highly concerned and perplexed) Becky . . . ?

GRACE:

Fool. But like I said, if the shoe fits, why bother taking it off?

REGGIE:

Becky? . . . . Becky? . . . . Becky? (Searching room to room.)

LIGHTS

ACT II

SCENE I

GRACE:

(Reggie and Grace have both fallen asleep on separate chairs in the living room. Becky attempts to sneak into the house without disturbing her parents' sleep. She is nearly to her room before her motionless mother stops her progress.) Three times in the last five days, Becky. Three times this week alone and there are still two more days left to go in the week. (Slowly awakening from her sleep) Why Becky? Why? What is it that you want? WHAT? Isn't a beautiful home with two loving parents . . . food in your stomach and clothes on your back enough to be thankful for? What else do you want now, Becky? What else?

BECKY:

I want to know if we can talk about this in the morning, Mama. I'm really quite tired right now.

MOTHER:

(Rising and approaching the child as she speaks) Tired? Tired? But of course you would be, Rebecca. You see just looking at the dirty dishes and walking past the filthy living room . . . and not to mention totally ignoring the mess that's thrown around from pillar to post in your own room, oh now that more than enough to make any normal person tired. Now couple that with HANGING OUT IN THE STREET ALL NIGHT LONG LIKE SOME

KIND OF COMMON STREET WALKING HOT TO TROT MAMA and I can see exactly why you're so tired girl!

REGGIE:

(Dazed and sleepy acting) Good Lord! What is it NOW? Can't I ever get just one (emphatically from mother to daughter) one . . . one decent night of sleep and peace in this house! Gracious. I went to sleep with you (to wife) fussing about her not being home. Now I wake up to both of you fussing because she IS home and not out there on the streets some place. What the devil is going on in this house?

BECKY:

(Affectionately and innocently) Hi, Daddy! (Goes over and hugs him.) Sorry (ugly face at mama) Mama woke you up with that loud voice of hers.

REGGIE:

Hey there, Angel.

GRACE:

Angel? Angel? Reginald how the devil could you ever fix your mouth to call that child "ANGEL' after what she just did (gestures to the unperformed tasks) . . . or should I say did not do today?

REGGIE:

Baby, listen. I agree with you that my little honey bunch disobeyed and didn't clean up like you told her to, but come on now, Sugar Plum, it's late and it really doesn't matter this time of the morning (glancing at his bare wrist) whether she cleaned her room earlier last night or not.

GRACE:

What the . . . (takes a deep breath and recomposes herself) what exactly do you mean, "It really doesn't matter?"

REGGIE:

Baby, it's late, okay. And all I'm interested in doing right now is getting some sleep and some peace and quiet.

GRACE:

Reginald, what the devil are you talking about? Do you not know exactly what time it is, man?

REGGIE:

Well, naw, I guess it's around . . . about . . . shoot I don't know. Got no idea really.

GRACE:

Well how about me giving you some kind of an idea, husband of mine. It's two fifteen in the A.M., man, and this street walking child JUST came strutting up in my house—like it's the right thing to do—just about five minutes ago! And you gonna tell me to just not say anything about it until later! I don't hardly think so. Not for one minute! Becky (to daughter) you get over there on that sofa and sit down 'cause you got some long and good s'plaining to do, child.

BECKY:

Daddy, didn't you say we could talk about this in the morning?

REGGIE:

Well yeah. What I said was . . .

GRACE:

Don't you EVEN try that junk with me, girl! I told you to get over there on that sofa and sit down. And the last time I checked I was just as much mama as he is daddy. So don't you EVER again go to your daddy to get him to overrule me just because you don't want to be disciplined.

BECKY:

That's your whole problem. You want to run everything. Can't nobody tell you nothing! Nothing at all. (To her father) And you'll so weak that you're willing to just sit back and let her strong arm you like you're just a little wimp or something. Sometimes I don't even know why I bother to even call you daddy. Maybe I should just call her both mama and daddy since she seems to run the show and you just seem to only run around in the show.

GRACE:

(Slaps Becky across the face.) Girl, don't you ever again use that tone or those words to address either me or your father. Now I think I told you twice to sit down and if I have to say it once more I'll knock you down and drag you across this floor and sit you up on the sofa myself. But you gonna sit on that sofa TONIGHT! (Child does not move. She engages in a stare down with mom. Mom starts to roll up her sleeves as if preparing to tussle.) So . . . help . . . me . . . GOD!

REGGIE:

BECKY! Sit down, Becky.

BECKY:

(Still staring at mom) I'll sit down alright. But one thing everybody in this house better recognize, and that is tonight was my last night ever again taking another lick off anybody living under this roof.

GRACE:

What you just say, child?

BECKY:

Ain't studdered and I ain't changed my mind either. And like I just said you better believe there ain't gonna be many more—NO more—slapping me in my face around here and getting a way with it. You can believe that. You don't know you better recognize . . . before folks have to memorize—after they eulogize and come expecting me to apologize.

GRACE:

(Completely unable to contain herself any longer.) Memorize! Eulo—. (Snatches Becky around by the arm.) You little street walking . . . (Does not finish before she has struck the child again. Child falls to the floor. Stares up at her mom. Then announces . . .)

BECKY:

It's on now baby. Bet up. It's on now. (Jumps up and charges at her mom. The two begin to tussle. The two are talking back and forth as they tussle. Dad tries desperately to break up the confrontation)

REGGIE:

Becky! Grace! (He is back and forth between the two.) Becky! Becky I said sit down over there now. Grace! Grace! This is your child for goodness sake! What the devil has gotten into you woman? Are you crazy? Your child! What's wrong with you, Grace?

GRACE:

Don't you dare ask me what's wrong with me after you stood right there and heard that child all but threaten me—AND you. A better question to ask is what's wrong with you, man? When are you going to quit being so much of the male in this house and become more of the husband and the father that are needed in this house?

BECKY:

You see? You see there! That's just what I told you, ain't it? Little Miss Know It Completely All. Can't nobody tell her nothing 'cause she already thinks she knows everything under the sun.

GRACE:

I have told you about dipping in adult business, Becky!

BECKY:

Oh so now I'm just suppose to stand up here like a tin soldier or something while you stand over there and talk about me like a stepchild or something, huh?

GRACE:

Who the devil's talking about you, Becky?

REGGIE:

Becky, I want you to sit down and just shut up while I'm talking to your mother.

BECKY:

Why I got to sit down and shut up? Say? Why can't she sit down and shut up? Much as she talks around here her mouth needs a break anyway.

REGGIE:

No more of it, Becky! No more! Now sit down and SHUT YOUR MOUTH! Now!!

GRACE:

Hum-m-mp!! That's exactly what happens when you love them so much that you spare the rod and spoil the child. Ain't nothing wrong there that a little bit of chastising on the backside won't correct.

BECKY:

That's all you know how to do, ain't it? Beat people! Slap people! Yell at people.

REGGIE:

I told you to shut up, Becky!

GRACE:

And I just told you Becky ain't gonna do what you say because you done spared the rod too long.

REGGIE:

Grace, I don't need you raising me, alright?

GRACE:

I'm not raising you! I'm trying to raise my child!

REGGIE:

No you're not! You're trying to make me feel guilty about not raising OUR child just the way YOU think I should.

GRACE:

Wrong again, Father Knows Best. I'm unhappy with the fact that you won't raise that rebellious child the way the word of God says you—a Godly man—are suppose to.

REGGIE:

Get off my nerves, GRACE!!

GRACE:

I'm not on your cotton picking nerves!

BECKY:

Yes you are. You're always on people's nerves. All you ever do is nag, nag, nag and get on everybody's nerves.

GRACE:

There goes that rebellious child's mouth again.

BECKY:

And there goes that know it all woman's mouth again too. Besides that what are you going to do about my mouth anyway?

GRACE:

I have had all I can take of this.

BECKY:

Oh yeah, now what?

REGGIE:

Becky!!

GRACE:

I bet you I'll beat your (as she bolts furiously towards Becky.) behind until you can't even remember this week. (a second struggle begins.)

REGGIE:

BECKY!! GRACE! (TRYING TO SEPARATE THE TWO) BECKY! STOP IT! STOP IT!! (SCREAMING TO THE STOP OF HIS VOICE) I SAID STOP IT RIGHT NOW AND I MEAN STOP IT RIGHT NOW!!! (DRAWS BACK AS IF PREPARING TO BACKHAND BECKY WHO BEGINS RE-APPROACHING HER MOTHER.) I SAID STOP IT BECKY. AND IF I HAVE TO SAY IT AGAIN, YOU'LL FEEL MY WORDS AND NOT JUST

HEAR THEM. NOW YOU SIT YOUR GROWN AND HARDHEADED BEHIND DOWN IN THAT CHAIR RIGHT NOW . . . (pointing directly at her as she prepares to speak but he cuts her off abruptly) and don't let me hear as much as a whisper out of you unless I ask you a question . . . and I mean it too young lady.

GRACE:

(Visibly upset and breathing very deeply. She is holding her chest. She looks back and forth from her husband to her daughter. She looks as if she wants to speak but can't. Her daughter glares at her menacingly. Then turns her back to her parents. Then softly . . .) Reggie . . .

REGGIE:

Pure hell! That's what this place has come to be. Can't get no peace on the job! Can't have no peace off the job! Can't have no peace at church!

GRACE:

Reggie . . .

REGGIE:

Can't have no peace in my own home. Can't have no peace in my car. Just can't have no peace period . . . NO PLACE!

GRACE:

Reggie (Growing weaker and still clutching her chest. Collapses on the couch. Father nor daughter pays any attention. They are both pre-occupied.)

REGGIE:

What is it, Grace? (No response. He is now more irritated.) I said, what is it, Grace? (No answer) Grace what do you wa—(turns and see her collapsed body with her hands on her chest lying sprawled upon the coach.) Grace? . . . . Grace . . . . GRACE!! (Quickly examines her for a pulse, dilated pupils, and temperature.) Oh my God. Oh my God. Oh Lord please help me. Don't . . . Lord please . . . don't . . . you can't let this be happening to my house too.

BECKY:

(Noticing the seriousness of her father's words lowers the magazine she is now reading.) What is it, Dad?

REGGIE:

Oh Lord. Lord have mercy.

BECKY:

Dad, what is it? What? What's the matter, Daddy? What's the matter with Mama? Dad?

REGGIE:

Call 911, Becky! Hurry up!

BECKY:

Daddy, I didn't mean to (point to her mother.)

REGGIE:

HURRY UP I SAID, BECKY! 911!!! It just may be too late for apologies now.

BECKY:

(Stunned and perplexed) Too late?

REGGIE:

(Snatching the phone and dialing the number himself) Operator. I need an ambulance quick!

OPERATOR:

(Voice off stage) Calm down sir. It will make it much easier to help you.

REGGIE:

Don't tell me to clam down! I need an ambulance. NOW!!

OPERATOR:

Sir, what is the nature of the problem?

REGGIE:

The nature of the problem is a possible massive heart attack. And I don't think my wife is going to last much longer if you don't hurry up and get some help over here right now.

OPERATOR:

The victim is your wife, sir?

REGGIE:

Yes. (Becoming irritated and impatient.) Yes. The victim is my wife. She's a 43 old black woman and (places his head on her chest.) She's barely breathing at all. (Grabs her arms and feels for a pulse) a-a-and her pulse is extremely weak too. It was stronger than this just seconds ago. I'm telling you she's fading fast! You've got to get somebody over here and quick!

OPERATOR:

And where is the victim, sir?

REGGIE:

2758 Glory Road, Hephzibah.

OPERATOR:

Sir, I've alerted the Willis Foreman Road Medical Center and the Center has confirmed that an ambulance is in route to the victim's current location with an ETA of approximately two minutes.

REGGIE:

Two minutes. Good. We'll be here waiting.

BECKY:

Daddy?

REGGIE:

Not now, Becky.

BECKY:

I killed Mama?

REGGIE:

Well, she's not dead yet. And with the help of God and the para-medics (nervously glancing at his wrist, forgetting he is not wearing a watch) she won't die any time soon either.

BECKY:

Daddy . . . I didn't mean to do this (music) . . . I mean . . . I really wasn't even mad. I was just fooling around with Mama, Daddy. Daddy you got to believe me . . . I didn't know this was gonna . . . .

REGGIE:

I told you, Becky. Not now. Just ain't a good time to talk about all that right now. Right now we just need to pray to God that your mama lives long enough to get to the hospital. Right now, don't nothing else matter at all. Nothing at all, Becky. Nothing. (Daughter begins to cry loudly. Daddy is holding his wife's hand. Music up. Siren can be heard in the background.)

LIGHTS

ACT II

SCENE II

(EM personnel are working frantically to save the mother's life. Father and daughter observing from beyond a large window.)

DR. MAROONY:

Pressure! Pressure! Keep the pressure constant. I need 30cc's of thrombolytics and start me two IV's stat, one of niacin and one of beta blockers—10 cc's each. Stat, nurse, stat.

NURSE GRACE:

How much, doctor?

DR. MAROONY:

Correction. You had better make that 20 cc's each nurse. What happened to her anyway? Anybody knows?

NURSE GRACE:

Twenty cc's of throms and niacin, doctor. Not exactly sure what brought on the attack. Family member called 911 ranting and raving to the attendant. Never said what happened. Just gave the symptoms of cardiac attack.

DR. MAROONY:

Here! We can go in right here. I've got a vein here. Needle! (Pause) Heart's weakening. Pulse is diminishing. (Examines her eyes quickly) Eyes fixated. Defibulators! Where's her husband? Anybody knows?

INTERN (ARNIE):

In the waiting area, Dr. Marooney. He wanted to come in but I told him he'd have to wait outside. Trauma is too emotional and serious to have family in the vicinity.

DR. MAROONEY:

Good work. Did you happen to ask if there was a history of high blood pressure or cardiac problems in her past or in her family's past.

ARNIE:

No time, Dr. Scott. Patient needed my attention right away.

NURSE HOLBET:

Ready to shock doctor.

DR. MAROONEY:

Stand back everyone. (To the nurse) Give her a shock and see what we get. (Nurse delivers the shock, then . . .)

NURSE HOLBET:

Nothing. No change. Signs are all the same.

DR. MAROONEY:

Let your heart be anxious for nothing. There's a lot more living left in you to do yet young lady. Stand clear! Another shock!

NURSE HOLBET:

Monitors looks the same, doctor. Oh, oh. Oh!! CORRECTION! BP rising slowly— but steadily. Heart rate climbing. Body temperature stabilized at 101.3. Respiration labored but consistent. (Pause and brief observation) Vitals are stabilizing and returning to normal.

ARNIE:

Good sign, huh?

NURSE HOLBET:

For the moment anyway. At least for right now we'll say she out of immediate danger; but she's no where near recovered or well. She's got the whale of a long and difficult recovery ahead of her I can assure you.

DR. MAROONEY:

Let not your heart be worried, Nurse Holbet. Never worry. Worrying is against the rules, you know. She'll be just fine, and you can count on that. And I can assure YOU of that as well.

NURSE HOLBET:

Pretty sure of yourself, aren't you, doctor? How can you possibly ASSURE me that she will be alright when you have spent only a minimum amount of time with her? You have no idea how this woman will be twenty minutes from now. So how could you be so coy and cavalier so as to make such a comment—such an assurance? All due respect Doctor, but I truly hope you don't walk out of here and go outside this room and spread that positive-thinking-feeling-fine mentality into the minds of those desperate family members out there. They deserve better, sir. They deserve to know the truth. Those poor people are going to rest all their hope and her chances for survival on your every word . . . so whatever you say to them, make sure it's something you . . . and they . . . can live with . . . regardless to what happens to her. Just tell them the truth sir. The truth.

DR. MAROONEY:

In the next twenty minutes her temperature will have fallen from 101.3 to 99. Her heart rate will rise again. This time a closer examination will reveal a congenial heart disorder that is dangerous and risky to repair, but not impossible. Minimal involuntary muscular responses will also be noted, which in itself is miraculous considering the severity of her condition as well as the lapsed time since the onset of the problem. She will be charted as serious but guarded. But through it all, she'll continue to hang on in there until her time for a full recovery has come—and that includes that heart disease by the way— And that . . . Nurse Holbet . . . is the absolute truth. And I would advise you to buy off into it as well.

ARNIE:

(Removing his gloves and mask) He's never wrong about these things you know.

NURSE HOLBET:

How would you know? You've only been interning here two weeks.

ARNIE:

Well, you're kindda right. The truth is I've been an intern HERE for just two weeks. (To the doctor) I'll get the orderlies to wheel her up to 4th floor B Wing. I think room 114 is still open. I'll have them assign her there.

DR. MAROONEY:

Good job. I'll go to up to the third floor and talk with her husband and daughter now.

NURSE HOLBET:

Doctor? How did you know she had a husband and a daughter here? I never said that. And who said they were on the third floor?

DR. MAROONEY:

After they left the chapel praying together, they stopped off on the third floor. The father thought this was a perfect time to show his daughter the nursery where he first laid eyes on her, and the patient room where he sat in a long blue hospital gown and mask and held her for the very first time.

NURSE HOLBET:

How would you know that? You mean you know this family?

DR. MAROONEY:

Yes, Nurse Holbet, I know this family, but not as you know them. Trust me. They'll be on the third floor once I get there. I promise. It's the truth. (Turns and exits)

ARNIE:

Like I told you, he's never wrong about these things. (Exits followed by EM staff members wheeling the mother to her new room.)

ACT II

SCENE III

(Daughter and father are strolling along the nursery. Their countenance is sad as they admire the new born babies through the nursery window. Suddenly from behind and out of nowhere . . .)

ARNIE:

She'll be just fine you know. (Becky and father are both shocked. They thought they were alone.)

REGGIE:

Who are you? Where did . . . (confused) . . . How did . . . . When did?

ARNIE:

It's okay, Mr. Baxter. Don't be startled. I'm Arnie. I'm a friend of Becky's. I know what happened, and I'm sorry Becky was late getting in tonight, which led up to all of this drama.

REGGIE:

Late getting in. How did you know that?

BECKY:

Arnie, why are you even here? And on the maternity ward at that! Why? You here to visit one of your friends or something? (Pointing to the new born babies) Huh?

ARNIE:

No. I just popped in to tell you not to worry. It won't do no good no how. Just count it all joy and never let your heart be heavy. That's all.

REGGIE:

What the heck kind of fruit cake are you, boy? And who the devil are you anyway? Listen, junior, in case you didn't know it, I've got a very sick wife upstairs. Any minute I could be paged over the public address system to report back to the floor just to be told that my wife just expired. And here you come "popping" up in here to tell me some foolishness about how it won't do me any good to worry over her anyway. You young people today—I don't even know you. Who is this clown, Becky?

BECKY:

Somebody I thought was a lot smarter than what he's shown me here tonight. I'm embarrassed to even say he's a fri—uh— an acquaintance of mine.

REGGIE:

You should be. And how did you know Becky was late getting in last night, er, this morning?

ARNIE:

I was with her.

REGGIE:

WHAT?

BECKY:

Not like that, Dad?

REGGIE:

Then what other kind of "with her" am I suppose to think when you come stepping up in my house around the same time as people who work the early shift leave for work?

BECKY:

He means, he was part of the gang . . . group . . . that I was hanging out with, Dad.

REGGIE:

Gang?

BECKY:

Group! Group, Dad! I said group!

REGGIE:

Don't you lie to me little girl! Don't you do it! That's exactly how all this got started in the first place. You lying to your mother. Haven't you learned anything at all. Haven't you? Do you think it's some kind of joke why we're here right now. Well it's not a joke, Becky! It's a matter of life and death, Becky. LIFE AND DEATH. Your mother's life. My wife's life. My best friend's like. My companion's life, Becky! But for Christ sake, child, it's not a joke. It's not . . . not . . . a joke. (Frustrated. Turns and walk away mumbling as he crosses the stage.) Why do I even bother? Why do I even care? Why am I sitting up here arguing with the very same child that just gave my wife of 24 years and her own loving, kindhearted mama a major heart attack. Now why would this surprise me? Why? Why?

BECKY:

That's not fair, Dad. I apologize. I told you this was all a mistake. I told you I was just being a brat. I told you that I just being spoiled. I never meant for any of this happen.

REGGIE:

Yes, you told me. You sure did young lady. You told me that non-sense over and over again. But did you tell that to your mother yet? Did you tell her your teary story between heart shocks or in the back of the ambulance in route here? Did you tell her how sorry you were while she was unconscious on the couch or did you whisper it to her as they rolled her out of the house on the stretcher?

BECKY:

DAD . . .

REGGIE:

No, Becky. Answer me. Tell me the truth child! When . . . did . . . you . . . tell . . . HER?? WHEN?? And if she dies, will she be any less dead if you were acting bratty than she will be if you were just being your normal mean and ornery self? (Becky begins to cry again.)

BECKY:

Daddy I didn't mean it! I didn't mean it! I didn't mean it!

ARNIE:

She's telling you the truth, Mr. Baxter.

REGGIE:

(YELLING) AND HOW DO YOU KNOW WHAT THE TRUTH IS? HOW? She's MY daughter. I conceived her. I was there when she was born. I changed her diapers. I taught her to ride her tricycle. I taught her to swim. I showed her how to climb trees and be a little girl. I took her to church. I strolled with her in parks and sat up on Christmas Eve nights waiting for Santa Clause to show up. I did. I did. Not you—you little wimp! I did all these things and more. And because I did I should know when my own child is being honest or dishonest with me. I don't need some young hip hop generation slick willy to tell me when my own child is telling the truth and when she's not.

ARNIE:

(Still totally calm) Your heart is anxious and filled with fear for your wife, sir. Please, release it. There's nothing you have in your heart right now can do to help you or your wife. Release it, sir.

REGGIE:

Becky, who is this boy?

BECKY:

Just let me handle him, Dad, alright? (To Arnie) I don't know how you found me here. And I don't know how you knew my mother was sick either. But

I thank you for your concern, support, and advice. Now my father and I would like to spend some much needed quality time together. So if you don't mind . . . please . . . leave us.

ARNIE:

Sure. Catch you later, Becky. Mr. Baxter, sir. (Exit)

REGGIE:

I don't understand you or the people you hang round anymore, Becky.

BECKY:

He's harmless, Dad. The most dangerous thing about Arnie is his humility followed by his gullibility.

REGGIE:

I don't care how harmless he is, that boy is still weird. I don't care what you say. Something not quite normal about that boy. Can't say what, but it's something . . . that's for sure. (Dr. Scott appears quickly from their rear.)

DR. MAROONEY:

Great news folks! (They both are startled.) Oops! Didn't mean to startle you.

REGGIE:

Seems to be the going thing with us tonight. Same thing happened just minutes ago with one of her friends, and now you.

DR. MAROONEY:

Well I humbly apologize for the both of us and to add icing on the cake I come bearing miraculous and wonderfully glad tiding for the two of you.

REGGIE:

(He and Becky rush over and each grab one of the doctor's arms.) She's okay?

BECKY:

She's gonna live?

REGGIE:

She's out of danger?

BECKY:

Can she go home?

DR. MAROONEY:

Hold it! Hold it! Hold it! Not so terribly fast here you two. There are still a lot of things to discuss and decisions to be made; but to answer your questions yes, yes, yes for the moment, and yes in the near future.

REGGIE:

How about we talk about all that other stuff a little later, doc, but right now you take us to see her? Huh? Can we see her?

BECKY:

Please?

DR. MAROONEY:

Alright. It's obvious neither one of you will hear a word I'm saying anyway until you have seen her, so come on, let's go take just a quick peek in on Ms. Baxter and see how she's doing? (Begin to exit)

BECKY:

How did you find us, Dr. Scott? No one paged us and we never told anyone else we were coming here. I mean in a hospital this size, it's just not likely that you would just run across us, especially on a ward like this. How did you just happen to find us here?

DR. MAROONEY:

There is nothing in life that "just happens," Becky. There is a purpose behind all things. Be it known to you or unknown.

BECKY:

My name. How did you know it? We've never been introduced. As a matter of fact, how did you even know we were my mom's family members? We could have been anybody's family.

DR. MAROONEY:

To someone else, you could have been. To me, you could only have been whom I was told you were.

REGGIE:

Told? By whom?

DR. MAROONEY:

There is set in time, a plan to reveal all things as you have a need and a desire to know. This moment is not that time. Come on, let's see how the newest patient in room 114 is getting along? (Exit)

LIGHTS

ACT III

SCENE I

(Next morning. Becky awakens from sleep. She and her father have remained at the hospital over night. Father is still asleep. Becky quietly rises and goes to visit with her mother. Just as she prepares to enter her mother's room, the charge nurse calls to her from behind the nurses' station . . .)

NURSE GRACE:

Your mother's still a little weak, Becky, so be sure you don't stay too long.

BECKY:

Yes, ma'am.

NURSE GRACE:

Becky?

BECKY:

Ma'am.

NURSE GRACE:

Are you faithful? Faithful, Becky? Are you full of faith that anything you ask can be done?

BECKY:

I don't know. I guess.

NURSE GRACE:

Then be it unto you according to your faith. (Nurse gestures a perplexed looking Becky into the room. Becky steps beyond the door, thinks, then questions herself.)

BECKY:

Hey, this is the morning shift. How does she know who I am and my relationship to my mother? And how does she know my name? (Turns and exits. She is about to question the nurse when she notices the nurse is not there.) Excuse me ma'am but . . .

NURSE STROWFORD:

(A different nurse looks up from behind the desk.) Yes? May I help you?

BECKY:

Who are you?

NURSE STROWFORD:

Perhaps that is exactly the question I should be asking you young lady.

BECKY:

I'm Becky, (Pointing to her mother's room) her daughter. (Obviously confused) Nurse . . .

NURSE STROWFORD:

Strowford. Betty Jean. I'm Nurse Betty Jean—BJ—Strowford. I'm charge nurse for the 7-3 shift. As I have been for the last seven years.

BECKY:

Nurse Strowford, all do respect, but could you tell me where the other nurse went that was sitting in that chair just a minute ago?

NURSE STROWFORD:

You've been here all night, haven't you?

BECKY:

Sure. But that doesn't tell me where the other nurse went to.

NURSE STROWFORD:

(Still working and barely paying her any attention.) Well it sure as the dickens tells me. It tells me you are nervous and tired and that you need to go home and get some seriously needed rest because you are about to begin hallucinating.

BECKY:

Hallucinating?

NURSE STROWFORD:

Easily done when you get real tired, anxious, and nervous at the same time. Just your body's natural reaction to a lot of unusual stresses all coming down on it at one. You'll be okay.

BECKY:

But where is she?

NURSE STROWFORD:

(Finally looking up from her writing.) Listen, tuts. I've been sitting right her since I came on shift at seven this morning. Right here. Reading charts . . . Preparing medications. Writing in charts . . . Preparing medications. Answering phone calls . . . preparing medications. I have not left my post for one minute except to move right there (Points to the phone) to answer the phone or to go right back there to get prepare more medications. Other than that, anybody's that's come or gone in the last (looks at her watch) hour and fifteen minutes, I've seen'em.

BECKY:

You mean there wasn't another nurse sitting right there in that very same chair just a minute ago?

NURSE STROWFORD:

(Stands up and turns around) Baby you see these? (Patting her large hips very firmly.) They've been plastered in this chair for all of 73 of the last 75 minutes of this shift. Now even though I'm dieting (Takes a bite off her donut and a sips from her coffee) I still don't see how you could really believe that another grown female could have been sharing this chair with me.

BECKY:

You've been there for more than an hour straight?

NURSE STROWFORD:

Getting close to an hour and a half now that I've been talking to you.

BECKY:

And you've seen everybody that's come in and out of here?

NURSE STROWFORD:

Everybody! That's my job, babe.

BECKY:

When did you first see me?

NURSE STROWFORD:

When you stepped out of . . . (stops and thinks.) Hey! You got by me didn't you? Good job, tuts. Not many people can boast about getting past old eagle-eyed Nurse Mavis. I guess that makes you kind of special. Here, have a donut for your effort.

BECKY:

No. No donut. And I didn't get by you either Nurse Eagle Eye. I didn't. There was another nurse there. I know there was.

NURSE STROWFORD:

Okay, sweets. You say you don't want a donut. No donut. You say you saw another nurse . . . alright already . . . you saw what you saw . . . or thought you saw . . . or hallucinated . . . or whatever. Just be sure you get some rest before much longer, alright? (Switches charts. Bites donut. Sips coffee.) Don't take fatigue long to take its toll on any of us you know.

BECKY:

Sure. Thanks for the words of wisdom. (Turns and re-enters the room. She is startled to find Arnie standing next to her mom's bed.) Arnie!! What the . . . Arnie, what in heaven's name are you doing here? And how did you get in here? I'm standing directly in front of the door, so I know you could not have walked in. Where'd you come from and why are you in my mother's room anyway?

ARNIE:

Well, in heaven's name I'm ensuring that your mother is doing just fine. And I got in here the same way most of her visitors do.

BECKY:

And how was that, Arnie? You certainly didn't come past me.

ARNIE:

Oh, Becky, now you're beginning to sound like that old lassie out there at the nurse's station.

BECKY:

What? She gave you a hard time too?

ARNIE:

No.

BECKY:

Then what are you talking about?

ARNIE:

Nothing. You just sound like her, that's all. (Quickly turning his attention to Becky's mother) But your mother's fine. Not to worry. (Becky looks perplexed by his words) Oh sure it's going to take the a little time for the body to catch up to the spirit, but she's doing just great.

BECKY:

You're very weird, Arnold. I have no idea how you could even say certain things. I mean, look at her, and the tubes, and the IV's and the all this medical stuff and you manage to slip in here somehow and just look at her for only a moment and declare to me that my mom's fine. You're weird. You're disrespectful. You're stupid. You're . . . You're . . . Just get out of my face Arnie and . . . Never mind, I know exactly how I'll handle this. (She bolts to the door. Exits. Storms over to the nurses' counter and begin raving . . .) Nurse Cobb I demand to know who gave Arnie permission to enter my very sick mother's room. He's not a part of this family and no family member placed him on the visitor's list. I am not at all happy with his presence in her room and I am demanding that you do not allow him to visit with her again! Is that clear? (The nurse lifts her head. Becky is shocked. It is the same nurse with whom she spoke upon initially entering the ward.)

NURSE GRACE:

Arnie was only doing his job, Becky. I'm sorry you're upset. I'll ensure to speak to him about the matter.

BECKY:

You-u-u! They said . . .

NURSE GRACE:

Yes. I know. But aren't you talking to me?

BECKY:

(Speechless) Yes.

NURSE GRACE:

I know what others say to you about me, Becky, but what do you say to you about me? There will be many opportunities for us to talk later. Visit with your mother right now. It's very important that you do. Go ahead. Talk to her. She's able to hear everything you say to her. This is your appointed time with your mother.

BECKY:

(Becky retreats back across the hallway. She re-enters the room. There is no Arnie.) Arnie! Arnie! Arnie! Man, this is wild! Arnie! (Becky goes over and sits next to her mother. She gently strokes her mothers head and hand then begin to sob aloud.) Mama, please don't die. Please. You can't. You can't do that to me. Please Mama. You can't leave me now. Who else is going to be there for me like you. Who else is going to love me like you? Who else is going to do for me like you? Who else, Mama? Who else? (Beginning to sob again.) Who? Who? Who else? You—You just can't go NOW, Mama. You CAN'T. I mean the house is a mess. Daddy's lost without you. And to tell you the truth, so am I.

GRACE:

(Extremely weak. Her speech is totally unexpected to Becky.)

You mean the only reason you want me around is to clean up after you and your daddy. (Becky jumps.)

BECKY:

Mama! Mama!

GRACE:

You still don't understand yet, do you?

BECKY:

Understand what, Mama? And how you know I don't understand whatever it is you're talking about?

GRACE:

No time to argue, baby. Mama's too weak right now. You just listen to me, okay? This battle ain't mine. And it ain't yours. This is a personal battle between God and Satan. And you nor I can win it. Only the power of God can win this fight.

BECKY:

Mama, what you talking about?

GRACE:

You want another mama in your life? Do you? You want one?

BECKY:

Mama! No, Mama. You know that. You're my only mama. Nobody in the whole world could ever replace you in my life. You know that, Mama. No matter how I act sometimes, you know I still love you.

GRACE:

Inspite of your ways and the way you treat me? Yeah, Becky, I guess it's pretty easy for any a pure misguided fool to see just how much you must really love me.

BECKY:

Mama . . .

GRACE:

It doesn't matter, Becky. You see my body has been lying here. But my soul's been walking around in Paradise. God has allowed me to sit in the company of his angels and to talk with them and they have made me know that this fight ain't even about you or me. You see this is a revenge fight. Kindda like those folks who are always going back in and shooting up the post office after they've been fired.

BECKY:

(Very perplexed) Mama, maybe you should just get some rest.

GRACE:

No, Becky, I know what I'm saying. I'm weak now, and I don't know how much longer I can stay with you, but while I can let me help you understand just what's going on with you. (Music) You're anointed, baby. You're anointed by God to obey His word, do His will, and to edify his kingdom. Now the devil show 'nuff don't like that. You see, the devil use to be God's right hand man (smiles) eons and eons ago. He was God's praise and worship minister. And God loved Satan's job. He loved it with all his heart, and he created Satan just to do the job which he—God—loved most, which was to give praise and worship to Him as the one and only true and ever living God. But the devil lost track of the truth about his job. He started to believe that his spiritual job and gift were his talents to command and use as he wished. And so he opposed God and lost, as did as those that followed him. They were kicked out of heaven into a place prepared just for them . . . a place called hell . . .

BECKY:

But, Mama, what do any of this have to do with me?

GRACE:

Just like you don't want another mama in your life, deep down inside Lucifer didn't want to lose his favorite thing either— his job; but he did. And then God created man to replace Lucifer and all his fallen angels. We took Satan's place in the trinity of angels—the warring angels, the messenger angels, and, of course, the praise and worship angels—that's us. It's like a child who's been the apple of mama's and daddy's eyes, then suddenly there's a new baby in the house and the new baby gets all the attention.

BECKY:

So you're saying the devil is jealous of us?

MOTHER:

Jealous and dangerously mad. We took his place. We took his job. We took his glory. We took power. And now he's determined to destroy those who replaced him and to make God sorry that he fired him. You're just an employee, baby. The fight is between the two employers. The employer of good and the employer of evil.

BECKY:

But what does this have to do with you being here?

GRACE:

I'm employed by the Kingdom of God, Becky. And when that become the case in anybody's life, the god of the kingdom of evil sets out to make them sorry they ever became employed by God's kingdom. He sets out to make their life miserable. He sets out to steal, kill, and destroy everything good in their life. He tries to break up their homes, their ministries, their families, the futures, and to bring division between them and their children. He's evil, baby, thoroughly evil, and he brings no good with him. He'll destroy all that we have just to show us that we are not going to serve God in peace.

BECKY:

You mean the devil will use me to destroy you?

GRACE:

The devil will use anything and anybody to destroy anything and anybody that is about God's work. Becky this heart attack was not about me. I'm safe in my daddy's hand. No weapons formed against me can nor shall prosper because I'm more than a conqueror and greater is He that is in me than he that is against me.

BECKY:

Then if it was not about you, then who was this heart attack about?

GRACE:

It was about you, Becky. God needed to get your attention, and this was His way of doing that. You needed time, Becky. Time with me . . . like right now. Time with your daddy. Time with your heavenly daddy. And time with . . .

BECKY:

What's the matter, Mom?

GRACE:

Becky, this is a very strange hospital. At least some of the members of the staff are. (Pauses) You know Arnold?

BECKY:

Arnold? A-a-a-ah! Mama, how do you know that . . .

GRACE:

Sweet young man? His fervent prayers are what pulled me through. I'm tired, Becky. I guess it's the medicine. I need my rest now. Just remember, Becky, this whole thing was never about me. It was always about you. It's just that the Lord had to use me in order to get your attention. I'm so tired.

So tired. So ti-i-i-i

BECKY:

Mom, are you going to be alright? Mom? Mom? Oh, God! She's coding again. Nurse! Help. Somebody! Help! It's my mom! Help! Help! (Medical staff ruses in. Becky is observing from a distance—tearfully.)

MEDICAL ATTENDANT:

STAND BACK! CLEAR! CHARGE! NO CHANGE! CLEAR! CHARGE! ONE LAST TIME. CLEAR! CHARGE! (MUSIC. BECKY IS TEARFUL. SOBS AWAY IN BOTH HANDS.)

LIGHTS

ACT III

SCENE II

(The action resumes in the family's home. No one is at home except Becky. She has showered and changed and is hard at work cleaning the house. Her efforts are obvious as the house appears immaculately clean and organized from top to bottom. She is finishing up the living room floors. Gospel music is playing in the background. Voice comes over the radio.)

DJ:

Ladies and gentlemen, we have a special prayer request today from a Mr. Arnold . . . er . . . oh . . . there's no last name here. No one seems to know how this note got here either. But that's not important. What is, is the prayer request. Arnold is requesting prayer for the mother of Becky Baxter, a close and special friend of his. To the Baxter family, we here at station W-L-R-D lift up the woman of your family before Elohim our God, and request the creator and keeper of the heavens to send his angels and command them to take charge of matters concerning this sister's illness and of this family. We thank you, Arnie, for that request and join you in declaring a complete miracle in this matter. Now ladies and gentlemen and all of you out there in our listening audience and under the sound of my voice, I invite you to join us in prayer as we pray during our period of musical meditation. (Meditative music plays. Becky sings aloud. She finishes her songs. Sits on the sofa and begins to talk out loud.)

BECKY:

Oh, Lord. Just look at poor little old me, won't ya? Me, Lord. Miss Mouth of the South, as . . . Mama . . . would say. The one whose never . . . EVER . . . at a lost for words. Now when I need words in the worst possible way, I . . . I . . . I can't fine any. I can't find the words to say what's really in my heart . . . and my head. I can't find the words to say just how I'm feeling . . . or why I even fell like I do. Lord, now I know why the pastor's always saying he needs a word from You. Well, anyway, one thing's for sure and that is things ain't gonna get no better unless I try, huh. So, Lord, here goes all I got.

VOICE:

Becky (she hears the voice and looks around), have no fear and be full of faith. Know that whatsoever you ask, if you can believe, even before you pray, know that I will do these things for you.

BECKY:

(Totally unbelieving in what she is experiencing) No-o-o. No. This can't be. I can't be having a conversation with . . . YOU? Can I?

VOICE:

I know what you have need of even before you ask, Becky. And I will give these things to you, but only according to your faith.

BECKY:

And that's what's knocking me for a loop, Lord. I mean, listen, I'm just a child . . . and I'm doing childish things. You know . . . like being rebellious . . . smoking marijuana . . . hanging out with my people . . . and all the stuff I do just so that I don't fit the mode of being a perfect little angel . . . a mama's girl . . . or anything like that. But, Lord, you know I never meant to give my mama a heart attack. You know that. Lord, I love my mama. She and my dad's all I've got. I'm not crazy, Lord. I know these people I call my dawgs can walk away and leave me just like that (snapping her finger.) But always . . . Mama and daddy are always right there. Lord, I love them both. Jesus, don't . . . please (starting to cry) Please don't let my mama die! Please Jesus! Please-e-e! Not my mama. God I couldn't live if I thought I had killed her (crying harder) No. No. No. God please don't let me be the death of my very own mother. (Sobbing) Oh God! Please don't, God. Please don't let my mama die! (She has not noticed her father entering. He is behind and reaches out and touches her on the shoulder. She is surprised by his presence.) Daddy! (Jumps up and hugs him)

REGGIE:

I saw Arnie at the hospital. He told me you left the hospital while I was asleep and that I would find you here.

BECKY:

Arnie? (Confused) I haven't seen Arnie since around eight this morning. How would he know where to find me?

REGGIE:

I can't answer that. I just know that he obviously knew what he was talking about. Said I'd find you here praying and cleaning the house. Looks to me like that weirdo was right about both things. (Goes over and sits down.) Truth is I didn't come all the way here from the hospital to discuss some adolescent kid who acts a little weird.

BECKY:

Yeah. You're right. (Sadly) How did you leave her? Dad listen . . .

REGGIE:

Becky, your mama . . . (Dad and Becky begin to speech simultaneously.)

BECKY:

What, Dad, what about mom?

REGGIE:

No. You go ahead and tell me what you had to say. Then I'll finish.

BECKY:

No, Dad, you first.

REGGIE:

No, Sweetheart. I insist. Ladies first. What is it?

BECKY:

(Very serious and concerned sounding) I want to know how my mom is doing, Dad.

REGGIE:

She's about as well as can be expected, baby. After all she did have a real serious relapse you know. And heart attacks are no joke—especially somebody me and your mama's age.

BECKY:

Yeah, that's exactly what I keep hearing. Dad, is she going to . . . to . . . to

REGGIE:

To what, Becky?

BECKY:

You know. Is my mama going to d.d.d . . . leave us soon?

REGGIE:

I am neither He who numbers her days nor am I the author and finisher of anyone's fate, Becky. In other words, I can't answer that question, Honey. You got to talk to the Lord about that. Only He knows the true answer to that question.

BECKY:

Why didn't you ask him?

REGGIE:

Because it's your question. Therefore you should ask it.

BECKY:

Daddy, if something does happen to mama

REGGIE:

You mean if she does die.

BECKY:

Yes. If she does go away (resisting the word die) . . . did I k-kill her?

REGGIE:

Becky, there is assigned to every man a number of days after which he has an rendezvous with eternity.

BECKY:

I know all of that, Dad, but did He assigned her that number of days only because he knew I would grow up to be an ornery, mean, disobedient child who would shorten her life by my behavior? Or was that just the number of days she would have gotten anyway.

REGGIE:

Why do you consistently ask me to explain God's decisions?

BECKY:

That's my point, Dad. Was this God's decision or was this a result of my rebellious attitude? Don't you see? Just because she's there with a heart attack doesn't mean it was necessarily her TIME.

REGGIE:

Huh. Time. Time. Time. Reminds me of a poem my eighth grade teacher made my whole class recite many years ago. I never forgot it. All those years.

BECKY:

How'd it go?

REGGIE:

It says, "Time is not a distance. Time is not space. Time is the course every man is given at birth to travel. Every man's time is different. Every man's course is different. No man is ever late nor early. He is simply on time in accordance with 'his' time. He never arrives nor leaves a station along his travel before nor after 'his time' assigns him to do so. And despite his will, he cannot nor will not accomplish any more nor any less than has been assigned to his time course for God knew he who would vigorously pursue the offerings of his time course when he designated and assigned such courses. Each course has been errorlessly plotted and assigned for the purpose of ultimately manifesting a pure and perfect will that is inconceivable to the minds of men which are late in their recognition, acceptance, and reverence of God's concept of time as it relates to man."

BECKY:

Wow!! That was beautiful, Dad.

REGGIE:

Thanks. Even though I had to learn it in school, it was your grandfather who wrote that. And now years later I'm still here wrestling with its truest meaning. (Knock at the door) Come in! (Arnie enters)

ARNIE:

Good evening, sir . . . Becky. Just thought you'd like to know that the misses is doing much better now. At the risk of sounding morbid, I must admit, sir, the doctors are absolutely baffled. Can't understand why two heart attacks like that didn't kill her on the spot. My non-medical answer, sir . . . if I may . . . just wasn't her time. (Becky and Dad look at one another.) Y'all be blessed. Mr. Baxter. Becky.

BECKY:

(Running to the door) Arnie! Arnie! (Gets to the door and looks both ways.) Where'd he go? There's no way you can get out of sight on this street that quickly. (Baffled) I can't quite say what it is, but I know there's something strange going on around here. I know there is. Dad, maybe we should pray before we head back out to the hospital again.

REGGIE:

Good idea, Becky. After all we can never pray too much.

BECKY:

Hey, Dad. Can we walk to the hospital this morning? I mean it's only about 15-20 minutes away on foot. And the walk will give us some quality time to spend together . . . like we use to. What say, Dad?

REGGIE:

Sure why not, baby. To be honest with you, I desperately need the exercise anyway. Walking, huh? Good idea, Becky. Save us a parking fee.

BECKY:

That's what I'm talking about! C'mon, Dad. Let's pray. (They kneel. Music.)

LIGHTS

ACT III

SCENE II

(The action takes places on the same street as the action in Act I Scene II. The group characters are the same minus the presence of Becky. The group is "smoking and joking" as Frankie notices Arnie's approach and signals his arrival to his peers.)

BLACKHAWK:

Well, well, well, well, well! Just looky what the almighty wind done (makes a wind-blown sound with his mouth) huffed and puffed and blew this way.

GINNIE:

What's sup, Arn? Where you been hanging all day dawg. Ain't seen you since you jetted out here some time back.

FRANKIE:

What's up, dog?

ARNIE:

Ain't been in nothing real special. Just out chilling and taking care of some . . . business. You know how that is. (Blackhawk hits the joint then passes it to Ginnie who hits it and passes it to Frankie who hits it and offers it to Arnie who nods no.)

BLACKHAWK:

Still a punk, huh? Freaking ma'ma's boy!

GINNIE:

Hey, where's my girl? Becky! Ain't seen her in a little bit come to think of it. Aye! Y'all got something going on, you and Becky? I mean y'all show nuff looked real tight the other night, dog. Hear what I'm saying?

ARNIE:

Well, that depends on who's eyes you were looking through.

BLACKHAWK:

Boy plea-a-se!!! You always got some off the wall way of answering people, you know that? That's one thing . . . one of many too . . . that I don't like about you.

ARNIE:

I call it like I see Blackhawk, not like you see it.

BLACKHAWK:

Then maybe I just need to help you change the angle you see things from.

ARNIE:

You can't do that, Blackhawk.

BLACKHAWK:

(Starting over to Arnie who seems to pay him no attention at all.) Bet?

GINNIE:

(Restraining Blackhawk with assistance from Frankie.) Yo! Yo! C'mon man. Lighten up, Hawk. Every time you two come within a hundred feet of one another we're on the verge of World War III again. How about a little peace this morning, man?

BLACKHAWK:

Well you better tell that little punk to watch his mouth then before I make him the quietest person in church this Sunday. (Folds his hands across his chest as if to say Arnie will be dead if he keeps it up. Arnie totally ignores Hawk's antics and continues with his conversation.)

ARNIE:

She'll be passing this way soon. (The trio look one to another in confusion.) Becky! She's with her dad. They'll be passing through here shortly in route to the hospital to visit with her mom who suffered a massive heart attack last night and another one this morning.

GINNIE:

TWO heart attacks?

FRANKIE:

What brought that on, Cuz?

BLACKHAWK:

Like he a doctor or something.

ARNIE:

It happened after the two got into a major argument after Becky left here and got home way too late last night, er, this morning.

BLACKHAWK:

How you know? You won't in Becky's house last night. As a matter of fact, you didn't even leave here with Becky last night. So how you know what you talking about? Say, how you know?

GINNIE:

Hawk's got a point, Arnie. Becky left here with me last night and you didn't walk with either one of us home. So he's right. How do you know what you're saying?

ARNIE:

Her mom's going to be alright, though. It's just a matter of faith. She's got the faith she's just got to be taught to have faith in her faith.

BLACKHAWK:

Oh my God! Here goes Mr. McGoo off the deep end again. Man why can't you just . . . you know . . . give people what they ask you for and no more. Why is every simple question turned into a mystery or a riddle with you? Don't you know yes and no and maybe and I think so and definitely and not hardly and other stuff like that? Why is everything a star wars memo when it comes from you? God!!!

ARNIE:

That's blasphemy, Hawk. (Blackhawk look at him quizzically) To use God's name in vain is blasphemy! You'd better watch that.

BLACKHAWK:

Naw! You'd better watch me you little arrogant punk 'cause I'm gonna kick your butt. I've had just about all of you that I can take!!

ARNIE:

(Hawk prepares to hit Arnie. Arnie remains still, calm, and composed.) That wouldn't be wise, Hawk. You could do more damage than good.

GINNIE:

(Ginnie steps between the staring pair.) Hawk, let it go. You know how Arnie is. Just let it go and forget about it. (Becky and her father have just approached the gang from the rear side in route to the hospital.)

BECKY:

Sup guys?

GINNY:

BECK!! BECK!! Sup girl? Where you been hanging all morning?

BLACKHAWK:

Yeeh! Blabbermouth here been spreading rumors 'bout you and your mom's balling it out after you fell up in the crib early this morning and ya mom like got hit with a big one (holding his heart), tracking with me, dog?

GINNY:

Yeah. He's right. It's all real. Oh yeah, this is my dad guys. Dad these are some of my . . . friends.

REGGIE:

(Looking about skeptically as they extend their hands in courtesy.) I see. Good to meet you all . . . I think.

GINNY:

It's all good, sir. Old folks always look at us like they don't know whether to shoot us or hug us. They just don't know what to make of us . . . but we're alright. Just kids.

REGGIE:

Becky, we've got to go.

BLACKHAWK:

Ease up, Pops. We just trying to rap with Beck-Beck for a minute. I mean we ain't seen her since she made that mad dash outta here last night.

REGGIE:

You mean this morning, don't you?

BLACKHAWK:

Last night. This morning. I don't know. You know, it's like the time just all starts running together all of a sudden.

REGGIE:

(Looking at Blackhawk smoking a joint.) It's no wonder. I can see why.

BLACKHAWK:

Hey! Gotta do what I gotta do. Don't knock this poor man just for trying to keep his head outta the water in this rich man's world.

REGGIE:

Rich man? What rich man sold you those drugs? Or made you come out her and stand on this corner and break the law (Pointing to him smoking on the corner.) What rich man ordered you to disrespect your elders or to destroy your own community, schools, and even your ownself? Whoever the richman was that did, I don't blame him, because it was the poor greedy man that says yes suh, yes suh, I'll do jest like you say suh so I can grow up and be just like you and take advantage of other poor people too. You'll excuse us, we need to get to the hospital.

BLACKHAWK:

(Jumps up and runs around to block Father's path.) Wo-o-oat! Wait! Wait! Hold up a minute old timer. I mean I ain't no book genius or nothing like that but I'm down with words enough to know when I'm being called a fool.

GINNY:

Chill, Hawk. Give'm respect now. They gotta go. Man's already done told you his wife is sick. What else he needs to say?

BLACKHAWK:

I ain't talking to you, Ginny; so just shut up.

GINNY:

Hawk . . .

BLACKHAWK:

Shutup, Ginny. Just shut up!

BECKY:

(Stepping between Hawk and her father.) Get out the way, Hawk. Didn't you hear? My mom's sick and . . .

BLACKHAWK:

Hey, girl! I don't care nothing 'bout my own mom let alone your mom or anybody's else. (She slaps him out of impulse. He draws his hand back to slap her back)

REGGIE:

You do . . . and so help me God this is the very last spot you're ever visit on planet earth—except your grave site. And that's a promise. Now get out of our way, boy! Now!

ARNIE:

You heard him, Hawk. Time's a wasting. Step off. And I can't ask you many more times either, Hawk. I said step off, big boy. (Hawk does so. Is obviously anger and distraught.) You two had better walk fast the rest of the way or you'll never make it in the 15-20 minutes you said you would.

REGGIE:

You're right. As a matter of fact we've only (looking at his watch) got a few . . . (looks up quizzically) How did you know we said we could make it to the hospital in 15-20 minutes?

ARNIE:

You're wasting time, sir. Your wife needs you now.

BECKY:

Come on, Daddy. We've got to make up for lost time.

GINNY:

I'm sorry about all of this. If there's anything at all I can do . . .

BECKY:

It's time like these that you get to see just who your real friends are. Leave the gang. Learn to pray and have faith in God. That's the best thing you could ever do for me, yourself or anybody else.

GINNY:

Thanks girl. (Hugs her)

BECKY:

(To Frankie) Goes for you too. (He gives her a nod and a thumbs up) C'mon Dad, let go.

GINNY:

What about him (Pointing to Arnie.)

BECKY:

I don't know. I just get this feeling that somehow he already knows that. I also got a funny feeling, some way we're going to run into you again at the hospital too.

ARNIE:

I wouldn't be surprised.

BECKY:

Me either. (She and dad begin to exit. Frankie and Ginny exit opposite direction. Blackhawk goes over and sits down on the corner. Lights a joint. Arnie quietly observes him for a short while then exits without speaking.)

LIGHTS

ACT III

SCENE III

(Scene is set in the mother's hospital room. The other two nurses enter Grace's room and discover Nurse Grace already there. She is busy at work in the patient's room and pays no attention to them as they stand mesmerized at her inexplicable presence in the patient's room. Nurse Grace eventually makes her way to the foot of the patient's bed where she retrieves her and reads from her chart. She suddenly breaks out in unrestrained laughter and begins dancing about the room waving the patient's chart as if celebrating.)

NURSE GRACE:

Hey! Hey, Hey, Hey, Hey, He-e-yy!!! Oh what a time we're in for today! Oh don't you just love days like this! (Singing) Oh this is the day that the Lord has made. I will rejoice and be glad in it! Oh, man, oh man, oh man! Boy it's these kinds of assignments that make me so glad I'm an (A highly perplexed and irritated Nurse Strowford abruptly interrupts her celebration by snatching the patient's chart from her hand and demanding . . .)

NURSE STROWFORD:

Who the devil are you?

NURSE GRACE:

Devil? Do you mean who the devil am I or who am I to the devil?

NURSE STROWFORD:

Listen, baby. It ain't a good day for humor so save your pathetic attempts at it, okay? All I need to know is who in hell are you and what are you doing in this patient's room?

NURSE GRACE:

Sorry, baby, wrong kingdom! Me and (still dancing) hell got nothing to do with one another. You're too far south (pointing to the floor then to the ceiling.) I'm more from up north! (Looking at the patient's chart) This one is really gonna be fun! A real wing ding doola! (Goes over and grabs Nurse 2 by the shoulders.) Don't you just LOVE these days. Oh I do! I just love them. I love them. I love them. (Singing and dancing about the room.) This is the day that the Lord has made. I will rejoice and be glad in it. This is the day! This is the day! This is the day that the Lord-d-d-d h-a-a-s m-a-a-d-d-e-e!!

NURSE HOLBET:

(Grabbing Nurse 1 by the shoulder and snatching her around.) Now you listen to me you tied little old witch!!

NURSE GRACE:

Witch?

NURSE STROWFORD:

You heard her, WITCH!! Now I don't know who you are or what you're doing here or even how you got here as far as that goes . . . all I know is . . . (stops and thinks) That's right. How DID you get here? I've been on that front desk since this morning, and I haven't done as much as blink. There's no way you could have . . . . ah-h-h-h . . . that's it! That's it?

NURSE GRACE:

What's it, baby? (Mockingly)

NURSE HOLBET:

You're that *nurse*.

NURSE GRACE:

(Humorously) Nurse? ME?

NURSE HOLBET:

You're the one that girl was talking about. But how did you get in here without being seen? And just how do I know you're really a nurse and not . . .

NURSE GRACE:

An imposter?

NURSE HOLBET:

Yeah.

NURSE GRACE:

A perpetrator?

NURSE HOLBET:

Right!

NURSE GRACE:

A sick minded psycho?

NURSE STROWFORD:

You said it, sister!

NURSE GRACE:

An angel?

NURSE HOLBET:

Like I said, spare me the humor baby. (Emphatically) Spare me the humor. I'll call security to get you out of here Miss No Name. We'll have you fingerprinted and profiled within ten minutes with just one phone. Guaranteed! (Heads to the door to call for security.) I personally promise that you will never see this unit again in your . . . (turns to address Nurse 1 and discovers she is no longer present.) Oh . . . My . . . . God! (She rushes over and examines the bathroom, then behind the curtains, then beneath the bed, then outside the door.) Oh . . . My . . . God! An angel? (The doctor enters but is unnoticed by the nurse who is busy starring off into space.)

DR. MAROONEY:

My goodness, my gracious! Why you look just like you just saw an . . . . well I won't say? How are you today?

NURSE HOLBET:

(Still in a trance.) An angel.

DR. MAROONEY:

Boy! Talk about giving yourself due credit.

NURSE STROWFORD:

Well it's just like I've always said. Somebody's got to give us a little bit of credit for all the good we do around here. (Notices Grace's IV is nearly empty.) Just like this IV. Just think what kind of a condition this poor critter here would be in if there weren't good nurses like me around to look after her.

DR. MAROONEY:

Well just when do you suppose you're going to start doing your job and looking after her, Nurse Strowford? Doesn't her IV need changing? And isn't it about time for you to start your med rounds? (Jokingly) And to just think— you're one of the better nurses here!

NURSE STROWFORD:

Jokes! Jokes! Everybody's a comedian now a days. She has about an hour to an hour and a half worth of solution left in that bag. It'll hold her until I get back from my round. I hope y'all can handle things in here for that long—without me—DOCTOR.

DR. MAROONEY:

Oh you bet we can. Like nothing you've ever seen before, Nurse. Ever. Just wait until you get back in here, you're going to be shocked out of this world.

NURSE STROWFORD:

Sure, Doc. That's the same thing my husband told me 34 years ago before I married him. Thirty four years later . . . I'm still waiting for the big shock

Actually, Doc, I'll tell you. I think all of you men are basically the same. Everyone of you.

DR. MAROONEY

Yeah? How so?

NURSE STROWFORD

Great at promising . . . Short on delivering. All of you. In that way, everyone of you is the very same. Alright, Doc. Gotta love you and leave you. I'm on my way to make rounds. Shouldn't take me more than 60-70 minutes. (Starts toward the exit.) Oh yeah?

DR. MOORNEY

Yes.

NURSE STROWFORD

Do a little bit of detective work and see if you can find out how Nurse Houdini managed to magically appear in here, why don't you? Who knows, Doc, maybe *that's* what going to shock me out of this world when I get back, huh? (Exits)

DR. MAROONEY:

Quite a character she is. But you have to love though. And I do.

NURSE HOLBET:

Doctor? There's something weird going on here and I can't figure it out. Alright. Here goes. The only way I know how to ask you this is to ask you straight out. (She takes a deep breath.) Doctor? (Dr. Marooney is checking over the patient's chart and seemingly is paying very little attention to either the nurse or her anxiety.) Doctor!

DR. MAROONEY:

Yes, yes. No need to scream, Nurse Holbet. I'm standing right here and I'm perfectly capable of hearing you know.

NURSE HOLBET:

Alright then, doctor. Here's what I want you both to hear and to answer for me. (She pauses then asks . . .) Do you believe in other forms of life? I mean . . . (frustrated . . . then blatantly . . .) Doctor, do you believe in angels?

DR. MAROONEY:

(Eating an apple while examining the patient's chart. Seems to be paying very little attention to her.) Uh-hum. Of course.

NURSE HOLBET:

Why?

DR. MAROONEY:

Do you believe in human beings?

NURSE HOLBET:

That's stupid! Because I'm human and I belong to the human race. Wouldn't it be rather dumb on my part not to believe in what I am?

DR. MAROONEY:

(Examining the patient and listening to her heart through his stethoscope.) H-m-m-m. I would say so. (Enters Arnie. The nurse is startled as she heard no sound nor saw any signs of outside light entering the room through an open door.)

ARNIE:

They're only about ten minutes away. Should I detain them in the lobby for say five or ten minutes?

DR. MAROONEY:

You are an intern in more ways than one. Let me give you a very important lesson right now. Remember, God's work never needs our intervention; it only needs our obedience. Wake her up, please. (Nurse Holbet is totally outwitted and now simply takes a seat and observes. Reluctantly she finally concedes to herself that she is witnessing something "extraordinary.")

GRACE:

Doctor. Why am I here? How-how-how did I get here? Wasn't I at home fussing with Becky? Where's Frank? My husband. Where is he?

DR. MAROONEY:

You're going to be just fine if you have the faith to be, Ms. Baxter. That I promise.

GRACE:

What are you talk . . . (tries to sit up and discovers she can't.) What's the matter with me?

ARNIE:

(Goes over to the bed and takes her by the hand.) It's time for your miracle, Ms. Johnson. God had to get your daughter's attention in order to deal with her before it was too late. And so he suffered your body to suffer two massive heart attacks. Between the two, he used your body and your voice to speak to your daughter in order that she might hear directly from Him and make decisions concerning her future. Now our mission is to help you receive your blessing and restore your health.

NURSE GRACE:

If there is no spiritual purpose, there is no earthly action, Ms. Baxter. Meaning, there is a spiritual purpose behind everything that takes place here on earth.

GRACE:

I was permitted to suffer a heart attack—isn't that what happened to me? (They all shake their heads yes collectively.) For what spiritual reason?

NURSE GRACE:

To recall your child's heart back to the love of God.

ARNIE:

So that your child would muster the strength to leave the streets and the gangs and to talk other young people whom Christ will use to build his kingdom here on earth into doing the same.

DR. MAROONEY:

To remind your husband that he is the Adam of your home and that he cannot relinquish those responsibilities as God has established him and him alone as the backbone, provider, and father of that house. And to remind him that should he permit its inhabitants to sway, their blood shall be on his hands on the day of judgment.

NURSE GRACE:

To test your faith.

ARNIE:

And to show you that God is yet alive, well and is still in the miracle working business.

NURSE HOLBET:

(As if in a dream) And to show me that there really are angels right here among us.

DR. MAROONEY:

(Tosses the chart to NURSE 2) You can destroy those records. They serve no purpose.

NURSE HOLBET:

Destroy medical records? I . . . I . . . I

DR. MAROONEY:

Sure you can. You see, after today there will be no record of her ever being here. No one will remember her. No one will have seen her. And nothing will exist to say that Sister Baxter shall have ever entered the doors of the Saint Mary's On The Hill Crisis Center. So you may as well. (She glances around, then concedes. She picks up the chart and rips it in half.)

ARNIE:

Good. Obedience is better than sacrifice.

NURSE HOLBET:

Your healing is on the way. (The quartet begins to dance about the room and sing loudly. The room has grown dim saved for the spot lighted area in which they dance.)

GRACE:

I want to dance with you.

NURSE GRACE:

Then get up out of that bed and come dance with us. Come dance, sister, dance! Come dance with us.

DR. MAROONEY:

By your faith . . .

ARNIE:

Come dance!

DR. MAROONEY:

By your faith . . .

NURSE GRACE:

Be healed!

DR. MAROONEY:

By your faith . . .

NURSE HOLBET:

(Jumps to her feet without control . . .) BE MADE WHOLE!!! (Notices what she has done. Covers her mouth shamefully and sits. Then jumps up and runs to join the dancing quartet.) BE IT UNTO YOU . . .

QUARTET:

According to your own faith.

GRACE:

I want to dance . . . . (thoughtfully) with angels.

NURSE GRACE:

Then do it, child of God. Just do it. All things are possible to those who believe . . .

ARNIE:

If you have faith but as the size of a single mustard seed, you can say to this mountain, mountain be thou removed and be thou cast into the sea and it shall be done. Where is your mustard seed of faith, sister? Where? Show me. Come dance with your angels.

GRACE:

(Struggling to get up. Falls back down. Dancing around her continues. Struggles more. And more. Finally sits up.) Mountain . . . be thou removed.

NURSE GRACE:

Speak to it sister! Sometimes our mountains get stubborn. They try to test our faith and try to convince us that they aren't going any place. But if you got that mustard seed of true faith . . . Speak! Speak! Speak to your mountain NOW! Speak!

GRACE:

Mountain . . . be thou removed (a little stronger than before.)

DR. MAROONEY:

They will be hewed up . . .

GRACE:

Mountain . . .

ARNIE:

And cast into the very sea!

GRACE:

BE . . .

DOCTOR:

Speak to it, sister . . . .

GRACE:

THOU

NURSE GRACE:

Command it to obey, sister.

GRACE:

RE—MOVED!!! (Pointing emphatically to the door.)

QUARTET:

Alright! Great! That's it! You're free now. You're free. You can dance now, sister! Come on and join us.

GRACE:

The devil ain't got no power in here. He's just a wimp trying to make me believe he's a strong man. But I got news for him. This little attack hasn't done a thing but made me stronger in the Lord. Just made me mad that's all. (Trying desperately to get to her feet.) Thought he was going to make my husband out of a wimp . . . my daughter out of street walker . . . and me a vegetable for the rest of my life, but I got just four words for him . . . (finally on her feet with the help of a walker that was near her bed.) YOU ARE A LIAR!!! As a matter of fact. I don't need this darn walker! How am I suppose to dance with my angels if I'm using a walker? Get thee behind me Satan and take this devilish walker with you!! Cause I'm dancing with my angel—THIS day!! (She throws the walker aside and begins to dance very gingerly . . . then more forcefully . . . then all out. The group is dancing and enjoying. The room is re-illuminated. Nurse 2 and Mother are dancing together so hard that they do not notice the angels as they smile and exit.)

REGGIE:

(Father and Becky enter as soon as the angels exit. They do not see them.) What the—Sweetheart, what on earth are you doing?

GRACE:

I'm dancing with my angels, baby. Hallelujah, praise the Lord, I'm dancing with my angels.

BECKY:

Mom, how could this be. I mean . . . You were . . . Just hours ago . . . I mean . . . . Oh my Lord what I trying to say?

GRACE:

(Begin dancing while she is talking) Listen, baby. Listen. All things work together for the good of those who love the Lord and are called according to His will and purpose. It is HE who takes that that was meant for our destruction and turns it into our good. Baby, if you know like I know, you'll grab you an angel's hand and just start dancing like you just lost your mind up in here.

BECKY:

Mama . . . what angels? If I saw one I probably would grab his hand and dance with him.

GRACE:

(Stops dancing and looks at her daughter.) Would you know an angel if you saw one, Becky?

BECKY:

I don't know if I would or not, Mama.

GRACE:

Then be careful how you treat all people, cause the Word says "Many have entertained angels unaware. And it also says, "Whatever you have done to the very least of these, you have done also unto to (pointing skyward) me." So dance, Becky. Dance. If you don't see an angel in the room dance with the ones in your heart. Dance with the ones in your dreams. Dance with the ones camp round about you night and day. But dance, child. DANCE!! Dance with your angel!

(LIGHTS)

(Minutes later)

NURSE HOLBET:

Whew!! What a time that was, huh?

BECKY:

I didn't know that was you. Shouldn't you be on your desk?

NURSE HOLBET:

Honey the desk can wait! Right now I feel like I should be on my feet dancing some more.

GRACE:

I hate to break the dance mood, but I got a question.

NURSE HOLBET:

Shoot it at me, baby.

GRACE:

If there are no records on me in here, how am I going to be discharged out of here so I can go home?

NURSE HOLBET:

If there are no records on you, then you've never been here. That means you're not a patient here now or ever was. Therefore, there is no reason why you can't just get up and walk straight out of here right now, is there? After all, a person as healthy as you are has no reason to be in a hospital anyhow. Now do you? And don't say yes, 'cause sick people can't dance like that!

GRACE:

I guess you're right. Then I can leave.

NURSE HOLBET:

Any time you like. But actually not until after you've made me one promise.

GRACE:

Speak it!

NURSE HOLBET:

That you'll never again stop dancing with your angels.

GRACE:

Promise *granted*. And I need that same promise from you.

NURSE HOLBET:

Promise granted. You know this entire floor will never be the same again.

BECKY:

It shouldn't be. No place where you've danced with angel should ever be the same again.

NURSE HOLBET:

You got that right. Especially my heart.

BECKY:

We're walking, Mom. Do we need to call . . .

GRACE:

Call what? Call on Jesus? Yes you do. Any other call is just a waste of time. Let's go family. (As they step into the hallway, a gurney is pushed by. Blackhawk is on it.)

DR. MAROONEY:

(Speaking quickly as the gurney is being hurried along.) He's overdosed and caused a major cardiac failure. He'll be extremely lucky if he's still alive by the time his parents get here. Nothing we can do for him.

BECKY:

Oh no!! It's Blackhawk!

ARNIE:

(Dressed as a hospital attendant pushing the gurney. Turns and is recognized by Becky.) He had an opportunity to dance with his angels too, but he didn't take it. He refused. And this is the consequence of his decision. The others are okay.

GRACE:

Hey! You're an angel! I just danced with you. He's one of my angels. I just danced with him.

BECKY:

Angel? Arnie . . . are you . . . an . . . (Blackhawk's last breath is heard leaving his body.)

ARNIE:

He's gone. It's over for him. (Silent pause) Even as you have done unto the least of these, you have done also unto me. Now you must answer for what you have done unto the least of these. (Becky looks away brief then glances back and notices that the doctor's, nurses' and Arnie's attires are all laying on the floor. She looks around quickly and notices no one. She runs to the window and notices the angels one on either side, one in front, and one in the rear of the black spirited Blackhawk flying skyward.)

BECKY:

Dear, dear, God. Arnie . . . An angle. Arnie.

REGGIE:

Becky, your mom's ready. Let's go home.

BECKY:

Coming Dad. (Looking skyward again.) He was an angel. Right here in my midst, and I never took the time to dance with him. I never took the time to dance with my angel. (Crosses to join mom and dad. Dad puts an arm around each as the trio exits.)

CURTAINS

DEFEATING THE DECEIVER

Ms. Collins enters, goes over and turns on the gospel radio station. She is obviously dressed for work, but has a housecoat on to protect her blouse from stains. She locates the station, adjusts the volume and exits. Subsequently the family enters onto center stage. Each appears to be emerging from his/her own bedroom. Dad, mom and sister are center stage and are impatiently awaiting the arrival of Jonathan. He is obviously delaying their regular routine and his parents are quite ready to depart for work. Dad goes to Exit R and mouths for Jonathan to come out and join the family. Jonathan is still slow but eventually emerges. He is visibly unhappy about having to join the family's morning prayer. He is very distracting and obviously quite stubborn and settled in his thinking. The prayer is concluded and the family members cheerfully embrace one another (except Jonathan) as they hurriedly exit one after the other to begin their busy day.

LIGHTS

An angel suddenly appears on stage as the music transitions into a worship melody. The angel dances about the entire house touching and anointing the house for the upcoming attack of evil that is on the way. When done, the angel exits and the music fades.

Setting: (Off stage in the black a sinister voice can be heard. Much pain and anguish can be heard in the background.)

VOICE

Go forth and steal. Go forth and destroy. Go forth and kill. Go forth my little demons. Go forth. Go forth and lie. Go forth and cause them to sin. Turn their hearts of flesh into hearts of stone and away from their God. Confuse their minds. Blind their hearts and destroy their hope. Go forth. Go forth. Go forth and prepare their souls for destruction and eternal damnation. I commission you, my demons of devastation and destruction and order you to go forth in my name and in my power. Go forth—and do my evil will. Go forth little ones. Go forth! Go-o-o forth!! Ha! Ha! Ha! Ha! (LIGHTS)

(Later that same evening.)

(Lights. Setting is the Collins' house. The appearance is mundane yet jovial. Ms. Collins and teenage daughter Kortashia are preparing for the family's dinner. Radio is playing. Off stage the DJ's voice can be heard coming over the radio.)

DJ

Praise God! And we thank the almighty for every single believer out there in radio land on this, another beautiful day that the Lord has made! I don't really know why I'm lead by the spirit to play this next selection, but I've always been told that obedience is better than sacrifice. And since the Spirit is leading me to play this next selection, I'll just be obedient unto Him who knows all things and humbly do as I have been directed. Y'all believers and praisers out there in radio land help me send up this next praise; it's called "God Is In Control." Doesn't matter the situation. Doesn't matter the appearance. Doesn't matter how impossible things may seem. We believers just look to the hills from which cometh our help, knowing our help cometh from the Lord who made the heavens and earth. So don't fret when the evil one brings your home or your business, or your children, or your marriage or your church ministry under attack. Just know that you know for sure that no weapon formed against you shall prosper and that all things work together for the good of those who love the Lord and are called according to His will and purpose. And if you know this then when the tests, trials and tribulations hit, it will a lot easier for you to respond to them by simply saying (Music starts) Sing along with us saints. Because I feel in my spirit that somebody is going to need to remember this before THIS night is out. Somebody will be tested, tried, and challenged by Satan himself THIS night, but the victory is already yours if you can just continue to send up the praises of this one song. (Music gets Ms. Collins' attention. She goes over and turns up the radio. Kortorsha shows an interest as well. The two join in as the music crescendos and takes them into a state of praise until the song finishes. Ms. Collins goes over and readjusts the volume after the song finishes.)

MS. COLLINS

Whew!! What a message in that song.

KORTASHIA

A-a-amannn!!! You ain't never lied!! Whew boy!! I like that!!

MS. COLLINS

Me too, baby. There's something more than just a good sound to that song there.

KORTASHIA

What you mean, Ma?

MS. COLLINS

Kortashia, it was just like God was sending me a warning . . . a message . . . almost like a prophecy.

KORTASHIA

I think you just really like that song, Ma. That's all.

MS. COLLINS

No it's not either. That is not all. The whole time that DJ was talking and the song was playing, it was as if God was summoning me to battle. It was like it was my battle cry.

KORTASHIA

(With humor) Mama, you getting ready to go to war, baby?

MS. COLLINS

You don't have much of a choice when the devil brings the war right to you, now do you?

KORTASHIA

O-o-oh Lord!! Don't go get all deep on me now, Mama. Remember, we're just talking now. Just talking. No need to go there on me right now. Chill out with all that deep stuff.

MS. COLLINS

(Very serious and stoic. Staring off into the distant.) Kortashia, that was a message sent from God. A revelation. A warning. I can't explain it any better than that. But there is no doubt in my mind, this house will see the glory of God and His manifest presence THIS DAY . . . but only if we can remember that it's God who's in control . . . and that He's working things out as they please Him. (Kortashia goes over and begins to set the table. Ms. Collins snaps out of her trance like state.) Kortashia, be sure you place a salad fork with each setting baby. I made a special salad to go with dinner tonight.

KORTASHIA

Um-m-m!! Sounds good to me. You know I love any kind of salad there is—special or not.

MS. COLLINS

Yes I know, and I do too. And so do your father and your brother.

KORTASHIA

Speaking of my overgrown brother, where is that lazy, hardheaded boy anyway? Knowing him . . .

MS. COLLINS

Ah! Ah! Ah! Don't you go there! Don't you dare! Don't you dare let a single negative word about your brother come out of your mouth! Not a single one!

KORTASHIA

Alright! Alright! Hey! I'm chilling. I'm chilling. Ain't like you got to say it twice or nothing. I'm cool.

MS. COLLINS

Good. Now finish setting the table like a good girl.

KORTASHIA

Wasn't going do nothing but tell the truth though.

MS. COLLINS

Kortashia Collins! Didn't I just tell you . . .

KORTASHIA

(Interrupting) But, Mama, look now. You know just as good as I do that the word says know the truth and

BOTH

(Joining Kortashia in quoting the scripture) the truth will make you free!

KORTASHIA

Right?

MS. COLLINS

That IS right, Kortashia. That's exactly what the word says. Glad to see you got *that much* word in you.

KORTASHIA

Aw-w. Come on now, Mama. You know I got PLENTY word in me now. That's one thing you know you don't have to worry about—me not having the Word in me. Hey, I know the Lord—because I know His word. I trust in the Lord—because I KNOW in His word. I praise the Lord—because I KNOW His word. And I believe and live by every syllable of His word that I ever read too. Oh, yeah, Mama, the girl *got* some word in her now.

MS. COLLINS

You go ahead then girl with your bad self!

KORTASHIA

But my brother . . . on the other hand . . .

MS. COLLINS

You stop right there then girl with your bad self! Now I just got through telling you that the power of life and death . . .

BOTH

Is in the tongue.

MS. COLLINS

Right! So don't you speak nothing against your brother that ain't pure and righteous and kind, and uplifting and full of hope and the wisdom of the Holy Spirit. You hear me? (No answer.) Tashia??

KORTASHIA

Yes ma'am. Whatever you say, Mama. Like the man just said on the radio, obedience is better than sacrifice. (Beneath her breath to herself.) Even though in this case I sure would rather do the sacrifice part.

MR. COLLINS

(Entering. Attired as if retiring from his office job for the evening.) Who-a-a-a!! Something smells GOOD up in this house!

KORTASHIA

Hey Daddy.

MR. COLLINS

Hi Sugar.

MS. COLLINS

Hi Baby.

MR. COLLINS

Hi Sweets.

KORTASHIA

No fair!!

MR. COLLINS

What's no fair, Kortashia?

KORTASHIA

I'm only your sugar, but Mama is your sweets. That means she's your sugar and candy and pie and cake and molasses and ice cream. She's everything sweet . . . but I'm . . . . I'm just sugar. No fair.

MR. COLLINS

Well, Tashia, Mama wasn't always my sweets either. She started out being sugar too. But over the years and through a lot of stuff . . . and changes . . . and situations, she slowly but surely became to me what she is now . . . my sweets.

KORTASHIA

Oh how PUR-R-R-TY. Make me just want to cry (fainting tears and wiping her eyes.)

MS. COLLINS

Child, as hungry as me and your dad are, if you don't HURRY UP and put those forks in place, you gonna cry alright, but it ain't gonna be because something is PURRRTY though.

KORTASHIA

Mama, how you know how hungry Daddy is?

MS. COLLINS

Because when you're your husband's sweets, you not only know his heart and his emotions and his spirit, but you also know his stomach. Now hurry up so we can eat girl. Hurry! Hurry! Hurry!

KORTASHIA

I'm hurrying. I'm hurrying! I'm hurrying!

MR. COLLINS

Where's Jonathan? He knows what time we eat dinner every day. He should have been here 30 minutes ago! This rebellious habit of his of doing just what he wants when he wants has got to stop . . . and now!

KORTASHIA

I don't know WHAT'S wrong with that boy, Daddy!

MS. COLLINS.

(Clearing her throat loudly to get Kortashia's attention.) Ah-h-h-h-h!!!!!

KORTASHIA

AND I ain't gonna say nothing—unless its pure and

MS. COLLINS

Positive

KORTASHIA

and Positive and . . .

MS. COLLINS

Righteous . . .

KORTASHIA

and Righteous—and

MS. COLLINS

Uplifting to the hearer

KORTASHIA

Yeah. And all that too.

MR. COLLINS

Yeah. Well good for you. But I'm gonna say something. (Ms. Collins goes to interrupt, but Mr. Collins won't hear it.) No, Belinda!!! I'm GOING to say something . . . and it's this one thing. And that is, something has gotten a hold of my son, and it's changing him in such a way that he can't see it. And since he can't see it, he doesn't believe it's really happening to him. And anything you don't believe is happening to you, you don't put up a defense against it. So then, without ever knowing it, you MAKE yourself even more venerable to what's really out to destroy you.

KORTASHIA

Because you don't SEE what's really destroying you.

MS. COLLINS

So you don't believe it really exists . . .

MR. COLLINS

So you don't fortify and defend yourself against it.

MS. COLLINS

It's all like a vicious and evil cycle.

MR. COLLINS

It IS a vicious and evil cycle, Belinda. A well planned out, well executed diabolically schemed cycle of destruction. (Suddenly changing the serious atmosphere) Let's not get too deep into all of this right now. How about some of this good smelling food. (Jonathan enters attired in typical street clothing.

165

He goes directly to the table and takes a seat. As he enters Satan's voice can be heard coming from off stage.)

VOICE

Go forth and cause much confusion in their homes and in their families. Go forth. Go forth.

JONATHAN

S'up folks?

MS. COLLINS

Jonathan . . .

JONATHAN

Yo!

MS. COLLINS

In this house . . . THIS house . . . EVERYBODY observes the family rules. It's called simple respect, Jonathan!

JONATHAN

Allite. Allite. Take a chill pill, Mama. I hear ya mouthing over there. It ain't like you go no reason to get all loud and stuff. Know what'um saying?

MS. COLLINS

Dinner is served in this house at 6:45 every day, Jonathan and not (checks the time) at 7:13!! We've done it this way every since you've been a small boy!

VOICE

Bring about discourse and confusion. Cause strife and destruction.

JONATHAN

Allite. Whatever. So what's in the pots today?

KORTASHIA

Now you can see why it's so hard for me to say something that's holy, and righteous, and uplifting about him.

MS. COLLINS

(Gesturing to her daughter to keep quiet. Then to Jonathan in a firm voice) Where have you been? (He pays her no attention. Does not respond. Sits erect from his slouching position and patiently sips its contents.)

MR. COLLINS

Son, didn't you hear your mother? She asked you a question. Answer her.

VOICE

Don't do it! Don't answer! Please! I love rebelliousness and family conflict.

KORTASHIA

(Out to the audience.) But I'm suppose to be able to say uplifting, righteous, holy things about him now.

MS. COLLINS

Kortashia!!!

VOICE

Oh I love it! I love it! I love it! I just love it when families are being destroyed. This is pure "hell" to me. Ha! Ha! Ha!

JONATHAN

Allite!! Out! Everybody happy now? I've been out, alright?

MR. COLLINS

No we're not happy!

JONATHAN

Well that's just too bad 'cause that's all I got to say. Now (inviting the family to the table) what y'all NEED to do is SIT down so we can THROW down on some of this good looking grub. (Sniffs the set table) Smells like fried chicken—like Colonel Sanders been up here, dawg! (Sniff) Can't fool a brother's nose none a bit. My nose is just like that bird on that one Fruit Loops commercial . . . the nose knows!

MR. COLLINS

No, Jonathan. It's more like a parent who sees what's happening and simply has to put his foot down in his own house. Grab your cap and jacket. You and I are going to take a little walk and have a long overdue man to man talk. Then I'm going to bring you back by the 24-hour clinic and have you tested for drugs, then we're going to church and ask the pastor and intercessors for a special prayer for you.

JONATHAN

Prayer?!?

VOICE

(Sounding desperate) Oh no. Not prayer. Please not prayer!

JONATHAN

Prayer?!?

KORTASHIA

You heard Daddy you big jarhead. He said (spelling it out) P-R-A-Y-E-R—Prayer!! What's the problem big man? You S-C-A-R-E-D—scared—to pray big brother?

JONATHAN

Who's talking to you squirrel face?

MS. COLLINS

STOP the foolishness you two! I don't want to heard another word of it out of either one of you!

VOICE

Stir up confusion and strife. Destroy their love and unity. Cause jealousy and hatred.

KORTASHIA

One thing for sure, YOU sure may not be talking to ME, but I sure know who's talking to YOU!!

MS. COLLINS

KORTASHIA!!

MR. COLLINS

Get your things, Jonathan. It's time for our little talk.

KORTASHIA

Long PAST time if you ask me.

JONATHAN

Hey! I told you to shut up, girl!

KORTASHIA

You don't tell me what to do! Just like nobody can tell you what to do!

JONATHAN

That's right!! 'Cause I'm grown!

MR. COLLINS

Jonathan I already told you once to get your stuff. Don't make me say it again!

JONATHAN

Don't you be yelling at me man!

VOICE

Confusion. Strife. Broken families. I love it! I love it! Seeking whom I may devour!

MS. COLLINS

Who do you think you're talking to?

VOICE

Yes! Yes! Father against son! Mother against daughter! Rebellion. Strife. Pain. Yes! Yes!

JONATHAN

You better step off old lady!

MS. COLLINS

Old lady? Step off? Oh I just know you didn't! No you didn't! You who I birthed! And wiped your stinking behind! And cleaned your snotty nose! And put clothes on your naked butt! And food in your empty belly! And did without so you could have! I KNOW you got better sense than to raise up in my face NOW and tell me to STEP OFF! Step off? You want me to step off? Huh? Is that what you want? You want me to step off, Jonathan Collins? Oh, I'll step off alright boy. I'll just step for enough off over to that stove so I can pick up a frying pan and knock the living . . .

MR. COLLINS

BABY!!

MS. COLLINS

Shedrick, you better talk to that boy . . . and right now. 'Cause I'll tell you what (rolling up her sleeves as if preparing to fight). He truly ain't got NO idea who he's messing with now. Tell me to step off like he's forgotten I'm his mama and not his equal. Like he thinks he's talking to some child or something. I bet you I'll grab hold of that skillet over there and KNOCK some remembrance back in his head.

KORTASHIA

Watch yourself, Mama! If you don't the devil in him just might try to make the Jesus in you say something about him that ain't good . . . and pure . . . and holy . . . and righteous. Uplifting to the hearing and stuff like that. You know what I'm talking about.

JONATHAN

All y'all just need to take a chill pill and get up off me in here! I can't even breathe in this old house for y'all up on me. Everything somebody do in this sanctified house, y'all got a "holy ghost" Bible declaring word for it.

VOICE

Go on say it! Say it. Don't fight my temptation! Be like Nike and just do it, will you?

JONATHAN

Well check this out. How 'bout I don't want no word no more!!! I don't need no holy ghost word for everything I do. So from now on y'all can just keep all that word none sense to y'all self. 'Cause if you ask me, all that Bible word stuff ain't nothing but just that anyway . . . a bunch of STUFF. Foolishness. That's all it is.

VOICE

YES!! YES!! HE SAID IT!! HE DOESN'T WANT THE WAY, THE TRUTH, AND THE LIFE THAT MEANS HE CAN ONLY WANT ME-E-E!

JONATHAN

And yo yo yo! Another thang while um preaching this sermon! I don't want no more worthless prayer either. What I need with prayer anyway? It ain't never done nothing for me in my life!

VOICE

Oh yes! He's making me so-o-o happy!

JONATHAN

And finally . . . (emphatically to each family member) Hear ye! Hear ye! Hear ye! I don't want to praise the Lord or have anything else to do with your God EVER again!! And you can tell Him I said so too. He ain't never done nothing for me that I couldn't do for myself anyway. So what I need Him for? Huh! I don't. So as of this night I'm cutting Him out of my life . . . forever. Matter of fact, it's a done deal right now. And none of y'all holier than thou saints of the most high God can talk me out of it either! And that's that!

VOICE

Oh, I've absolutely hit the jackpot with this one. I must congratulate my little demons on their superb work!

JONATHAN

I don't want you for my daddy no more. I don't want you for my mother no more. And the truth is, you little HOLY thing, I ain't NEVER wanted you for my little sister anyway. (Kortashia shrugs as if to say who cares.) So get this. I'm not your child anymore! (To his mother) I'm not your child anymore. And I'm not HIS (Pointing skyward) so-called child anymore either. And I ain't your brother no more either little Ms. Jesus Christ!! And you want to hear the cherry on top of all these flavors of ice cream?

VOICE

(Energetically) I do! I do! Tell me! I want to hear!

JONATHAN

I ain't ever gonna live in this sanctified house NO MORE ever again . . . where I have to hear all this foolishness about the word of God and the power of prayer all day long every single day. So now you can cook less food . . . clean one less room . . . and (knocks a plate from the table onto the floor) set the table for three and not four 'cause I'm outta this house for the rest of my life.

MR. COLLINS

You pick up that plate off of the floor right now, Jonathan.

JONATHAN

Don't you step to me, Dad! I'm warning you now because if you do it'll be an ugly day in the neighborhood.

MR. COLLINS

Don't you even try that foolishness with me boy! Now you pick up that plate off the floor NOW! (Being restrained by his wife as he attempts to make his way to his son.)

JONATHAN

You pick it up yourself CHRISTIAN MAN! I'm gone! I'm outta here. Later for all y'all . . . Christian family. Much later!!

VOICE

CHECKMATE!! Ha! HA! HA! Now I got him just where I want him. Good job my little demons! Good job!

(Car horn and tires can be heard blowing and screeching. Ms. Collins runs to the door. Looks out then frantically turns around and announces . . .)

MS. COLLINS

OH MY GOD!!! JOHNATHAN WAS RUNNING ACROSS THE STREET AND WAS JUST HIT BY A CAR. IT LOOKS REALLY BAD FROM HERE!! QUICK SHEDRICK DIAL 911! QUICK! QUICK! (Kortashia and Ms. Collins run out of the house to the accident scene. Mr. Collins completes the call then quickly follows them to the scene.)

VOICE

Yes . . . yes. I've got him just where I want him. Ha! HA! HA! HA! (LIGHTS/ MUSIC)

INTERMISSION

ACT TWO

SCENE II

(Offstage voice can be heard communicating with the hospital's emergency workers. Flashing emergency lights and sirens can be seen and heard during the communication.)

This is ambulance 4175 in route from 6875 Cuyman Street to your location with an approximate ETA of two-three minutes. Be prepared to receive an 18-21 year old black male. Medium build. Approximately five feet eleven inches to six feet one inch. Weight, approximately 175-185 pounds. The individual was struck by a speeding vehicle while crossing Cuyman Street. The victim is in serious condition and appears to be suffering from substantial internal injuries. His BP is low and fading fast. Cardio is faint and fading as well. Breathing is highly labored. Internal bleeding and damage are apparent. Again present ETA is approximately two minutes. Suggest you have a complete medical team on standby. This guy's definitely going to need it . . . and more!

As the lights come up the ER staff has received Jonathan from the paramedic team. They are working frantically to save him. His family nervously awaits the doctors' report. They are seated in the adjacent patient waiting area.)

DOCTOR

Stat! Nurse! I need an IV started on this boy NOW! Move it, nurse! Move it!

NURSE

We're doing all we can doctor, but nothing seems to be working for him.

DOCTOR

Try it again. The other arm this time.

NURSE

Yes doctor.

DOCTOR

I need a BP and pulse rate. What does it look like? Somebody come back with something. I need an answer! This boy is fading fast!

NURSE

Heart stopped, doctor. If we don't shock him now, we'll lose him for sure!

DOCTOR

DEFIBULATORS!

NURSE

Defibors ready!

DOCTOR

STAND BACK!! ALL CLEAR!! HIT IT! AGAIN. AGAIN! (Flatline monitor sound can be heard.) C'mon. C'mon. You can do it kid. Don't give up. C'mon. ALL CLEAR!! HIT IT!

NURSE

AGAIN DOCTOR?

DOCTOR

(PAUSE) No use. Put'em away. We did all we could. I'll go tell his parents. (Exits. Music: No Weapon. Re-enters stage area where family members are waiting and praying.) Mr. and Ms. Collins?

MR. COLLINS

(Anxiously) Yes, Dr. Longly.

DOCTOR

Mr. and Ms. Collins . . . I don't know what else to say except we did everything we could . . . everything we knew how to do . . . but it just didn't work for him. I'm sorry.

MR. COLLINS

You mean . . . my son is . . .

MS. COLLINS

Don't you say that! Don't you do it! Don't you say one negative thing about that boy. God said with long life have I satisfied thee . . . and I'm gonna take God at his word—REGARDLESS of what it looks like in the natural. Now I don't know about you, but I remember somebody asking the question, "Can these bones live?" And I remember somebody else asking, "Whose report will you believe?" And still somebody else asked "Is there ANYthing too hard for God?" Now I don't know about you, Shedrick, but personally, I don't see this as a termination of life situation. What I see here is a golden opportunity for God to show that He's still God even when medicine and science and man and technology have reached their wits' ends. Oh my God! I feel a Lazarus spirit coming up on me. And I need to impart it into my son. So I'm going in there and give to that boy such as I have. It may not be silver and it may not be gold. But I'll tell you this. What I DO have has more value than silver and gold together. I've got the resurrected spirit of the true and living God inside of me. I've got anointing, favor, grace and faith. I've got peace, assurance and Holy Ghost power. And now is the time for me to pass all of this on to my son. Now if you don't have the faith to call him back, you need to stay here until he and I get back out of that emergency room. Because I'm believing just like Abraham. "Me and the lad are going (pointing to the ER Operating Room) yonder, but by the power and anointing of the HOLY GHOST WE SHALL RETURN!"

MR. COLLINS

Baby, listen . . .

MS. COLLINS

I'm listening, Shedrick. But if you ain't saying what I hear God saying in my Holy Ghost filled spirit, I'm not hearing it!

KORTORSHIA

Mama is right, Daddy. You taught us that the power of life and deaf is in the tongue. You taught us that if we believed we can have anything we ask the Father for. You taught us that it was the deceiver who came to steal, and kill and destroy us, but Jesus, you said, came that we might have life and have life abundantly. That's what you said, Daddy. Isn't it? Isn't that what you told us?

MS. COLLINS

Now don't you be no fair weather Christian, Shedrick.

MR. COLLINS

Fair weather?

MS. COLLINS

You heard me loud and clear, Shedrick. Fair weather Christian. Meaning it good to TALK about the power of life and death being in the tongue until there comes a time for you to speak life back into the dead. Where is you faith now, Shedrick?

MR. COLLINS

My faith is right here where its always been.

KORTORSHIA

Then use it, Daddy! Use it. Now *is not* the time to start doubting the God who saved you and because of your prayers sanctified your wife and daughter. You can't start to doubt the God that healed you of cancer NOW. You can have no doubt in your mind that whatsoever you ask the Father, it will be His divine pleasure to give it to you. He already told you that no good thing will He withhold from those who believe in Him and call upon His name. Come on, Daddy. Not now. Don't let the devil play games with your faith at a critical time like this.

MS. COLLINS

These and greater works shall you do in my name. What *these* did Jesus do, Shedrick? He healed the sick. He said you'd do that too. He cast out demons, and he said you'd do that too. He gave sight to the blind, he gave hope to the lost, he healed the sick AND HE RAISED THE DEAD! Didn't he? Didn't he, Shedrick? And he said you'd do that too!!

MR. COLLINS

That's the word.

MS. COLLINS

And he said these SAME THINGS AND GREATER THINGS will YOU do, Shedrick by the power of the comforter whom he prayed to the Father to send in his place. Now do you believe him or not Shedrick? Don't you be one of those of little faith. Not at a time like this. The Bible says that if you have faith the size of a mustard seed, you can speak to the mountain and tell the mountain to be thou removed and the mountain will obey. Now you taught me all of this, Shedrick. And now it's time for you to take your faith to another level because we've got a mountain to go in there and move! Now, I'm asking you, man, are you one of a little faith or are you one of great faith? Our son's eternal destiny is depending on your answer. Life and death, Shedrick. Life and death. Heaven and hell. Paradise or purgatory. Now what do you say?

MR. COLLINS

We want to go in right now and pray for our son, Doctor. (To his wife) Thanks, Baby. I must have lost my sanctified mind there for a minute.

MS. COLLINS

That's alright baby. That's what I'm here for, to under girt you.

KORTORSHIA

Don't forget, Daddy. The mind IS the battleground of the spirits.

MR. COLLINS

Doctor, is it okay if we go in and pray with him now?

DOCTOR

Sure it's okay folks, but I just don't want you to go in expecting to come out with something that just can't be.

MR. COLLINS

Doctor, all due respect, but my family and I stayed out here in the waiting area, allowing you to do what you've been prepared and commissioned to do, and that is to doctor on people. Right?

DOCTOR

That's correct.

MR. COLLINS

Not one time did we interfer with you conducting doctor or medical business, right?

DOCTOR

I must say, that is also correct.

MR. COLLINS

Then just give us permission to go in and pray over my boy and don't try to work in an area in which you're not qualified. You be the doctor; we'll be the intercessors. Now is it alright for us to go yonder (looks at his wife and slowly points to the operating room) so that we can bring our son back here?

DOCTOR

Mr. Collins . . . have it your way, but I would feel so much better if you would just voice a more reasonable expectation. What you're hoping for is humanly impossible.

KORTORSHIA

Our hope isn't in a human, doctor. Many things are impossible with man, but with God, ALL things are possible.

DOCTOR

I guess I would feel much better about it if your father were to say that you were all going in to pray FOR your brother and not WITH your brother.

MR. COLLINS

(Interjecting as if to say I've had enough) No sir! We're going in and pray WITH him. It's not over 'till God says it's over, doctor . . . and right now God is saying I send you forth to pray with this, my child, at such a time as this for the purpose of rescuing his soul from the clutches of the adversary and returning him to Me. God's still got work on that boy and through that boy. Now all we need for God to start His work is your okay for us to go in there and start our work. Don't worry about not understanding what we're saying, doctor because the scripture tells us that God himself will confine the wisdom of this world and turn that which seems stupid into a spiritual sensation. He'll take that which appears to be sure death and destruction and turn it into a unique recovery. He'll take that which defies logic and turn it into a decisive victory over the adversary. My wife is right! I can feel the very spirit of Lazarus rising up in my belly. I feel God's anointing at work in my hands. I can sense the unmistakable presence of the Holy Ghost all over my body. I can see heaven's angels coming to escort me to my place of duty. The angels are here. The Holy Spirit is here. Miracles are here. Deliverance is here. Resurrection power is here! And they have all shown up here for one purpose and one purpose only and that is that they may escort us into the room where our son's body now lies so that they may manifest in no uncertain way the pure and miracle working power of God the Father. Now hurry up, doctor. Aye or Nay. Tell us something—and quick! 'Cause right now you've got all of heaven on hold. Legions of angels are waiting for you to say yes or no. The power of God himself is waiting for you to say yes or no. Now we just need to hear it from your own lips. But before you answer you better remember this. You just be a doctor. Don't try to play God. You've done all you can do. And we appreciate that and thank you for it. But now—now—now is the time for the irrepressible and all powerful might of God himself to show up and show out and to let everybody know He's still in control. So what do you say, Doctor? What do you say?

DOCTOR

Mr. and Ms. Collins, I know how difficult it is for you to accept this situation as it appears. But the sooner you force yourself to come to grips with the reality of what has happened here tonight—and I do know that it could take a little time—after all, it does take longer for some parents to accept the death of a child than it does others. But I just don't want to see you set yourselves up for additional pain and disappointment.

MS. COLLINS

Doctor, all due respect. But maybe you didn't hear us as well as we heard you. We heard your report. And I appreciate you for giving me that natural report. But as you were busy giving me man's report, God gave me a supernatural report AND assignment. And while I respect that M.D. behind your name, I hold the highest respect for the D that follows his name—El Elyon, G-O-D of everything. Now El Shadai has spoken into my spirit and has given me His divine orders and my assignment, and all I need you to do is to let us and the Holy Spirit have that room for just a few minutes—'cause if God said it—it is so!! You see, Doctor, this is nothing but a weapon, and God said that no weapon—no car accident, no rebellious spirit, no critical medical situation, no family problems—no weapon.

MR. COLLINS AND KORTORSHIA

No weapon!! They can't work!

MS. COLLINS

No weapon formed against me shall prosper. At least that is the way I like to it, Doctor, because that's exactly what the truth that I stand on, believe in and live by teaches me.

DOCTOR

As you wish, Mr. and Ms. Collins. I wish you success with your . . . er . . . prayer . . . As I said before, I know how difficult it is for parents to accept the untimely death of their children.

MR. COLLINS

Doctor? Just stand back and behold God's salvation at work. I promise you, by the time we get through in there, you going to have a different opinion about medicine verses prayer.

DOCTOR

As you wish. One thing I'll never do . . . that's stand between a family and its God. I'll have my staff vacate the room.

MS COLLINS

Get ready, baby and you too Kortorshia, 'cause the warfare is just about to go into high gear now! Get your armor on and get God's word out of your spirit and put them on the tip of your tongues cause we're about to go into the enemy's camp and TAKE BACK what he thought he had stolen from us. You ready?

MR. COLLINS

(He nods) Every step of the way!

MS. COLLINS

You ready?

KORTORSHIA

(Kortorshia nods) You know me, Mama. I've been waiting for a chance like this to whip up on the devil's head with the word of God, the faith of Abraham and the power of the Holy Spirit for a long time. Oh yeah. OH YEAH! Me and the Holy Ghost are through with all this talking. We're ready to be about my Father's business.

MR. COLLINS

Alright then family, let's touch and agree and remember this one thing (Song: He's In Us All). That is when we're done petitioning the heavens and the Father himself, we WILL have whatever we say as long as we believe in our hearts. Can we agree in the spirit on this? Can we walk into this battle separate in body but one in the spirit? For us to win this war, we've got to be of one accord, of one mind, petitioning one God for his supernatural assistance in this one situation. Let's go into the enemy's camp and take back what he stole from us. (They begin praying fervently as sound is faded.)

INTERMISSION

SCENE III

(Setting: Hell. Jonathan's spirit has just arrived in hell. He is perplexed and has no idea where he is no how he arrived there. He is very visibly tentative. Satan is seated at his big desk, feet propped, engaging in a highly jovial and seemingly satisfying telephone conversation. Screams and sounds of anguish and pain are heard in the background. Satan's phone call is abruptly interrupted when he notices Jonathan's arrival.)

SATAN

We got him? We deceived him too? Oh what evil news. What a kingdom I'm going to have some day. (Hangs up. Phone rings immediately rings again.) Yes-s-s. Mary Hatchet? She yielded to that simple temptation? Oh-h-h. (Pauses. Responding to his demon on the other end.) No wonder, she'd stopped praying and fasting, huh? She what? Oh she didn't fall for that old trick again, did she? You mean she actually began to look at the situation and circumstances and took her eye off (nodding skyward) Him? (Pauses) Became discouraged and stopped reading her word too? Well you know what I always say . . . it's either know THEE word or fall for MY word. HA! HA! HA! This is too much fun! I just love it when I get those "use to be strong Christian believers." Whatever happened to the believers who "walk by FAITH and not by sight?" Oh-h-h how wonderful! Just sends red hot heat waves down my wicked spine. (Finally notices Jonathan) A-h-h-h!! Yes! Yes! I see I have a new arrival. Let me holler at ya' later. Too-loo! (Hangs up) Jonathan, my boy! How good it is to see you.

JONATHAN

(Looking at Satan as if confused and half frightened.) W-w-who the devil are you?

SATAN

(Mimickingly) So far you're right! (Jonathan looks more confused) Why John-John . . . er you don't mind if I call you John-John, do you? I think it's such a cute form of your real name. Anyway, it's me! ME!! You know! Your adversary. The destroyer. The great deceiver. The father of all lies. The fallen star. It's me!! Lucifer!!! (laughter; Jonathan reacts); and I would like to welcome you to—hell— your new home. How do you like it so far? Don't worry. I know you haven't seen all of it, but once I finish your newcomers briefing, I'll take you on a personal tour myself!

JONATHAN

Lucifer? The devil?

SATAN

In all my splendor and glory. (Lucifer strikes a pose. One of his evil fingernails falls off.) Shoot! It's no wonder they call this place hell; (trying to force the nail back on, doesn't notice Jonathan's reaction to the word hell) nothing ever works right down here. (Suddenly remembers the huge diamond ring he's wearing. Flauntingly.) Like my new ring? Well, actually, I had one of my demons to possess a little boy who traded me his soul for this diamond ring (admiring the ring as he speaks). Then I had my demon to lead him out in front of a speeding car . . . like I did you right after you'd finished rebelling against your parents. Anyway the car hit him and killed him. Now guess what? (Very proudly) Now I have both the spiritual replica of his greatest possession . . . and his soul—forever!! Man, that's really hitting the jackpot; wouldn't you say so, John-John? But then, too, what does it profit a man to gain the whole world . . . yet lose his soul . . . . to ME . . . (Laughter).

JONATHAN

(Totally shocked. Speaking largely under his breath.) The devil. Lucifer.

SATAN

Oh please, Jonathan (gesturing energetically) don't be so distant . . . so formal . . . for evil's sake. And don't call me "the devil" either. It sounds so . . . so . . . well . . . descriptive. I like Lucifer better. It gives me a real name. A real identify. Kind of like John-John does for you. (Suddenly gets what he thinks is a good idea.) Hey, that'll be sweet, won't it? Lu-Lu . . . . you know . . . for me . . . short for Lucifer. (Jonathan does not respond.) Ah-h-h!. You don't look too pleased with it. To be honest neither am I. Come to think of it Lu-Lu sounds more like something you'd call a 75-year-old, denture wearing, gray haired great grandma. Don't you agree? (Decisively) Lucifer is good.

JONATHAN

Why did you do this to me? Why? Why'd you (Phone rings. Satan's hand goes up briskly interrupting Jonathan's questions. Satan answers.)

SATAN

(Sounding more serious and upset than when he was talking with Jonathan.) Hold that thought, Jonathan! (Into the phone) Yes-s-s. What? (Suddenly becoming serious) What do you mean you can't destroy him? Intercessory pray? Oh. There's no way we can get around those prayers and still get to him? Listen smart-mouth, don't you preach to me, I know EXACTLY what the fervent prayers of the righteous do, okay? Don't forget who I once was. I haven't always been stuck down here you know! (Pause). Hm-m-m. Nonsense! Absolutely nonsense! I won't hear of it! I've trained you well on my tactics and my missions. Now if you expect to remain employed in this evil kingdom you'd better get up there to earth and win me some souls. SOULS! SOULS! Do you understand that? I need SOULS. Corrupt souls that have perished without—you know who's (nodding toward the sky) grace and righteousness and forgiveness. I need souls and it's your job to get them for me! I didn't deceive you and have you cast out of heaven with me just so that you could come here and lounge around on some South American beach you know. So get busy you little evil thing and do your diabolical job! (Slams the phone down.) How does he possibly expect me to fill up hell—which I'm enlarging daily—if I don't get souls! Kill! Steal! Destroy! That's all! That's a simple enough non-changing operational concept! Isn't it? Steal, kill and destroy. How much easier can I make it? (Suddenly remembering Jonathan's presence.) Oh yes!! John-John! What were we discussing? Oh, yes! You were asking how did you end up here in hell with me, right? (Jonathan nods agreeably.) Oh, well, that's simple, Jonathan. You chose to.

JONATHAN

CHOSE? Are you crazy? I never chose to come to hell!

SATAN

Sure you did.

JONATHAN

You really are the father of all lies aren't you? You must be nuts! No one is his right mind would choose to come to hell.

SATAN

Sure they would. As a matter of fact, ANYONE in his own right mind would naturally choose to come to hell. Why, John-John? Because your NATURAL mind is enmity against (pointing) Him. Your NATURAL mind is carnal. It has no desire to do the will of (nodding upward) On the other hand, ANYONE who has had his mind renewed or has in him the same mind as (nodding upward) your buddy upstairs does, would choose those things that would land you in his home. Remember? "Be ye transformed by the renewing of your mind." And THAT is one of the greatest mysteries that Christians do not seem to understand. There is a reason that the mind is the battle ground of the spirits. Your mind is where either He or I win or lose you. Now do you understand my little servant?

JONATHAN

Don't you call me that! I'm not your servant!

SATAN

Suit yourself, but even you ought to know that this ain't the place He (pointing to the sky) was talking about when He said He was going away to prepare a place for you. Up there is where His servants are. Down here is where mine are . . . but . . . go ahead, Jon-Jon— suit yourself.

JONATHAN

(Pitifully) But I never meant to choose to come here.

SATAN

But choosing is the only way one gets here. No one ever MAKES anyone end up there (points to the sky) or here. It's all a matter of choices. See John-John I tempt (offers drink. JJ refuses)—but you decide. I offer (offers cigarette, again JJ refuses)—but you decide. I even persuade (removes and offers diamond ring, refuses)—but you decide. (Serious tone) Jonathan, I seek whom I may devour—meaning I study people (pulls out huge folder he has maintained on various individuals as he explains) and find their weaknesses. Then I develop specific plans on how to attack them at their weakest points at their most vulnerable time. (Tosses the folder on his desk) Then I give that assignment to some of my demons. They leave here with the assignment, return to the earth realm and plant thoughts and situations in the minds and paths of those whom I have sought. But, Jonathan, ultimately—you— choose your own eternity. He (pointing upward) or I simply reward you for the choices you made. Oh and by the way, John-John, let no man say that when he was tempted he was tempted of . . . you know who. For . . . HE . . . tempts no man.

JONATHAN

No! No! You're lying to me.

SATAN

(Flashing the three fingered Boy Scout's honor sign.) Scout's honor, Jonathan! You never had to make one bad or evil choice in your entire life. NEVER. You chose to. Remember Jonathan? "Now unto Him who can keep you for and exceeding abundantly beyond all that you could ever ask or think according to the powers at work in you!"

JONATHAN

NO! NO! You MADE me do the wrong things. You MADE me do them. YOU made me end up here! You did this to me.

SATAN

(Very slowly and lovingly) John-John. How pathetic you—and your childish temper tantrums— are. Can't you see it yet? It's as clear as this lovely wart on my nose.

JONATHAN

See what?

SATAN

I never MADE you end up here or any place else. I never FORCED one decision off on you. I never made you do one single thing—right or wrong. I only made it POSSIBLE for you to do wrong things. I only created situations wherein choosing wrong actually looked like a more beneficial choice to you. I only brought ideas, imaginations, desires, thoughts, and emotions to your mind. Then based upon which ones I brought to you, and what was going on in your life at the time, I whispered certain suggestions to you; but, JONATHAN it was you and not I who in the final analysis CHOSE what you would do. And with each choice you made, you were choosing your eternity.

JONATHAN

But I didn't know.

SATAN

Study, Jonathan, to show thyself approved. AND!! If any man lacks wisdom, let him ask of the Father who givest liberally. AND!! He told you that He prayed the Father to send you another comforter, which was the Holy Ghost (shutters as if the very words leave a bad taste in his mouth) and that He would lead and guide you into all truth and understanding. You are without excuse, Jonathan. Hell is simply your choice.

JONATHAN

But I'm too young to die and come to hell.

SATAN

And I saw standing before the throne, John the Revelator wrote in the book of Revelations, the great and the small, and each was required to give a full account of what he had done in the flesh.

JONATHAN

But you influenced me.

SATAN

Yes!!!. But then so did Martin Luther King, Jr, but I see you haven't chosen to lead any Civil Rights Marches lately. So did Harriet Tubman, but I never saw you choosing to lead anybody to freedom either. Michael Jordan influenced you. Got any Gatorade, McDonald's or Haines underwear commercials to show for it? What about NBA championship rings? Dale Earnhart influence you, but you never bothered to enter any NASCAR races. As a matter of fact, Jonathan, you haven't even bothered to go get a driver's license. Your days of mercy are over forever, Jonathan. Welcome to the halls of justice.

JONATHAN

So all my life you've only been deceiving me.

SATAN

Thus my title—the great deceiver.

JONATHAN

All my life you've been lying to me.

SATAN

(Proudly sporting himself about) The father of all lies.

JONATHAN

I never believed that you really existed. I thought you were some kind of religious fairy tale or myth. But now I see you are real. (Pensively) You destroyed me and my life and even my future.

SATAN

I come but for to steal, kill and destroy.

JONATHAN

They were right then.

SATAN

Who? Your parents? Sure they were right. Parents are nearly always right.

JONATHAN

Aw-w-w man! Just think. I thought all that stuff they were telling me about you was nothing more than just a big bunch of religious history that didn't apply to me and had long outlived its usefulness to mankind. Little did I know. I would never have ended up here if I had only listened to them.

SATAN

Precisely! Children obey your parents in the Lord for this is right. Yet yours is such a familiar story. I've heard it millions and millions of times. I must warn you though, it tends to lose its emotional appeal after the first 200 million times or so.

JONATHAN

Then God's word really is true.

SATAN

(Kneeling and bowing.) NO-o-o-o!! NO-o-o-o!! NEVER!!

JONATHAN

Never? Never what?

SATAN

NEVER call (pointing) *His name* in this place as long as you're down here. Where do you think you are, in heaven or some place kid?

JONATHAN

Why are you on your knees?

SATAN

Because at the sound of HIS (pointing upward) name EVERY knee shall bow and every tongue shall confess the HE and only HE is Lord of Lords.

JONATHAN

Even you too?

SATAN

Of course me too, dummy! Isn't that obvious? (Still worshiping. Speaking between bows) Who's in heaven and who's down here in this smelly, molten non-air conditioned sweat box? Who rules over heaven and who was kicked OUT of heaven? Of course me too!!

JOHNATHAN

Oh yeah. I never thought about that.

SATAN

(Agitated) Did I die rise with all power in my hand and ascend into the heavens? Do I hold the keys to both kingdoms in my hand? Have I prepared a lake of fire and eternal damnation for Him . . . or Him for me? (Getting back to his feet) Anyhow, let's not talk about all that stuff right now. Too depressing. It makes me feel so-o— . . .

JOHNATHAN

(Sensing Satan's weakness and his strength.) Little? Intimidated? Ashamed? Weak? Exposed?

SATAN

Thank you John-John, but that's more than enough adjectives to let me see that you got the point. I get your message. And it's not true either.

JOHNATHAN

So it IS true!

SATAN

How do you know?

JOHNATHAN

Because you're the father of all lies. You would never tell me the truth about something like that. You ARE little . . . you ARE ashamed . . . you ARE weak!

SATAN

SILENCE!!

JOHNATHAN

Silence? You've fooled me all my life. You've lied to me all my life. You've deceived me all my life. And now here I am in hell with you and you are telling me to be silent! What's gonna happen to me if I don't? Will I have to go live with the buggy man?

SATAN

I SAID . . .

JONATHAN

You said WHAT, Lucifer? What exactly did you say? I said God and you . . .

SATAN

Oh no not again! (Kneels and starts to worship.) I just told you not to ever call that name in my kingdom again.

JONATHAN

My God!

SATAN

Oh boy! Good thing I never moved, 'cause I'm sure tired of getting up and down and up and down like a yo-yo.

JONATHAN

(Moving about talking in amazement to himself) Even in hell He rules. That's amazing! God has no less power . . .

SATAN

Not again! I may as well just have a snicker bar 'cause it don't look like I'll be going nowhere soon.

JONATHAN

in hell than he does anywhere else. He is as much . . .

SATAN

No! Don't say his name. Plea-a-a-se don't say his name. Be a sport and give a devil a break. (Begins to stand slowly.) Man, shoot. If I had known I was going to be on my knees this much I probably wouldn't have bothered to rebel while I was in heaven. (Sudden shaking and loud rumbles. Jonathan is shocked and frightened.)

JONATHAN

What's that?

SATAN

Oh no! It's the fervent prayers of the righteous! They're shaking the very pillars of hell. They're destroying my strongholds. They're casting down my wicked empires and my spiritual wickedness in high places. (*Looking upward to the earth.*) Oh please, PLEASE stop praying. P-L-E-A-S-E!!

JONATHAN

You're crying. Lucifer . . . you're crying. The devil is crying.

SATAN

Wouldn't you be crying if you had spent year after year seeking to destroy someone and now all your efforts were being destroyed right in front of your face? Wouldn't you cry if you had gotten angels to abandon their creator and be kicked out of heaven, and you'd trained them as your own little evil demons and given them your own special assignments and now those strongholds that I set up generations ago are being destroyed because somebody is praying the prayer of faith or the prayer of petition, or the prayer of consecration, or the prayer of prosperity or intercession . . . or whatever kind of prayer? How would you feel if you'd been around for countless years waiting on the *right* member of the *right* generation of the *right* family so that you could destroy the next generation; and all of a sudden here comes some consecrated, faithful, full of the word prayer warrior who just prayed your stronghold down like it was nothing. (*The voices of his parents can be heard praying fervently*)

JONATHAN

I know those voices. That's my family's voices. They're praying for me. Even now as I talk with you . . . my parents are praying. They are believing God . . . YEAH! YEAH!! PRAY MOM!! PRAY DAD!! PRAY TORSHIA!! YOU'RE TEARING HIS KINGDOM DOWN. YOU'RE DESTROYING HIS

STRONGHOLDS! YOU'RE DEFEATING HIS DEMONS! PRAY!! PRAY FAMILY PRAY!! PRAY ME UP OUT OF HERE FOR GOD'S SAKE!!

SATAN

No! No! Not again!

JONATHAN

Family please . . . pray for me. (Pause) Believe. That's what they are saying. Believe and confess it NOW . . . and it shall be so. Believe. Now I get it! I'm not dead! And I'm not in your powers. Hell is not my home. My life isn't over yet! God . . .

SATAN

See, that's why I didn't even bother to move because I knew he was going to do it again!

JONATHAN

only allowed me this visit with you in order that I may see you, your home, and the truth about the universe's greatest liar and deceiver. Now I know, I really do have to go back up there and make better choices. I can't come here and be with you for eternity. I can't.

SATAN

Are you a fool? No one leaves hell. No one! You're only deceiving yourself. Once here—forever here.

JONATHAN

Lucifer?

SATAN

Yes.

JONATHAN

(CALMLY BUT WITH CONFIDENCE.) I denounce you.

SATAN

You what?

JONATHAN

I denounce you and I declare HIM (pointing to the heavens) to be the most high in all things.

SATAN

And you said all of that to say?

JONATHAN

I said all of that to say I thank my parents for planting the word in my heart. And the word says that in my time of trouble I can call on . . .

SATAN

I know who. I know who. Just don't call on His name (pointing upward) right now though, 'cause my knees are hurting some awful right now. Not use to being down on them, you know.

JONATHAN

and the word says He will deliver me out of the hands of mine enemies.

SATAN

Yeah, but it didn't say out of hell.

JONATHAN

Hell is my enemy and so are you.

SATAN

John—John, I'm your friend. You CHOSE to come to hell where I am. Remember?

JONATHAN

Let me tell you what I do remember, Satan. I remember my parents teaching me that if I confess with my mouth and believe in my heart that He is Lord of Lord and God of God and that he did through the power of his holy spirit raise His son from the dead then I shall be saved. And right now I am confessing and believing and declaring Him to be Lord of all. (Violent trembles and screams are heard. His parents' prayers are heard again in the background.)

SATAN

You know I'll never let you go.

JONATHAN

You have no choice.

SATAN

How will you ever get back to earth? A taxi perhaps?

JONATHAN

Thanks, but I'll follow my guardian angel. That way I won't have to worry about making any wrong transfers.

SATAN

You think this is all a joke!

JONATHAN

No. I think this was all a warning that God

SATAN

I AM SO TIRED OF YOU DOING THIS TO ME!!!!! (Falls down and begins worshiping)

JONATHAN

Good! Now you just stay there, and by the time you get up I'm sure I'll be someplace back in the earth realm. By the way it was really good to meet you. Now at least I know how real you are. (Turns and starts to walks out) Oh, Lu-Lu, Lucifer, fallen star, deceiver or whatever name you're going by—that wart on your nose is most definitely THEE most unappealing and ugliest thing I ever saw. By the way (recalling the reports on Satan's desk) let me check out those reports on your desk. (Starts to examine the contents.) Brian Baker? That's my neighbor! Melanie Carter! I know her. She goes to school with me. And . . . d Jonathan Collins . . . (Jonathan does not see Satan who gotten up from his knees and is approaching him from behind.) Can be used to destroy the entire Collins family. Weak in faith. No relationship with the Creator. Full of doubt and has no prayer life. The perfect tool to use to destroy the entire family. You mean you weren't just after me? You mean you were using me to destroy my entire family (Just as Jonathan prepares to turn around to face Satan, Satan launches forward and grabs him. Putting one hand over his mouth.) AAAHHH!! I told you that I would never let you go. I told you that I'd win and that you would spend eternity with me in hell! Didn't I? Didn't I, Jon-Jon? Ha! Ha! Ha! I win again!! I always win!! Ha! Ha! Ha! (Suddenly the fervent prayers of the family can be heard coming through.)

MR. COLLINS

Come on family. Press in. Press in. We're at the point of the storm before the calm. Don't give up. Don't doubt. Keep pressing in. Heaven has heard our cry and has already dispatched an angel to stand guard over him. I can feel it in my spirit. (Family prayers are still heard) Pray! Pray family! Press into the throne room of God. Press!

MS. COLLINS

You can't have my son, Satan. God said you can't. I command you to turn him loose. I command you to let him go! I command you in the almighty name of Jesus to loose your holds and ties on his mind and his spirit and his body. ANGELS, I dispatch you to the pit of hell to intercede for my son. Take him back from the enemy!

KORTORSHIA

Legions of angels, stand as guards watching out for his soul. Let no corrupt power have dominion over him. I order you to go into the depths of the pit of hell and to bring my brother back.

MR. COLLINS

Call him, son. Call on the name of Jesus. He's the only power that can free you from your situation. Call him! Be not afraid . . . but be bold in your confidence in the power of the almighty one. Call him. (Jonathan wrestles free of Satan. Suddenly he starts running about the stage trying to escape. Satan is right behind him.)

SATAN

I'll catch you yet. You will not get away from me! I'll get you Jonathan. (Suddenly an angel appears in hell. He is clad in all white and has his sword drawn. Jonathan sees him and suddenly rushes to him. He stands behind him and peers around him at a speechless and stunned Satan.) I'll get yo—OOOUOUU. Ouou. What the . . .

ANGEL

I am Gabriel and have come to return Jonathan to his proper place. (Jonathan licks his tongue at Satan.) I have not come to destroy you, Lucifer. But should you seek to deter heaven's mission, I have the Father's consent to destroy all of hell and its inhabitants. I am empowered with the same power that the savior brought with Him when He destroyed your works upon the earth.

SATAN

I don't want no parts of that. Boy! That's like walking right into a nuclear bomb explosion. Awwww shoot! What the heck? Who cares? Take him! There'll be plenty of more! Plenty of more whose parents are not saved . . . don't pray . . . and don't know . . . (pointing to the sky) Him. Take him and leave my evil dungeon to me and diabolical demons. This is no place for you goody-good angels. BLAH!

ANGEL

Jonathan, you are ordained by God . . .

SATAN

(Kneeling and worshipping) Not you TOO.

ANGEL

To return to earth and to testify of what you have witnessed here this day

JONATHAN

But who's going to believe this story? Man you can't even put this on Ripley's Believe It Or Not.

ANGEL

You job is simply to obey the Father . . . and nothing more.

JONATHAN

And that I'll do for the rest of my life, Gabriel. I promise. Gabriel, may I see just one more thing before I leave hell.

ANGEL

I am here to protect you. (Satan makes a disgusting face. Jonathan return to the desk and starts to review the files once more.)

JONATHAN

Erica Smith . . . Joshua Miller . . . Pastor Ike Ward . . . Vera Washington . . . Seth Henderson. (To Satan) You've really done your homework, Lu-lu. You've got enough information on everybody on earth to launch an attack at will.

SATAN

And I will. In time. In my own evil way and in my own evil time. I will.

JONATHAN

You mean you are really going to try to destroy these people and their heavenly works and rights.

SATAN

Not only do I seek to destroy them, I seek to even destroy the seeds of their unborn sons and daughters, Jonathan. Don't forget my mission and the whole reason I exist. (Slowly rising as he speaks.) My mission is simple. Steal. Kill. Destroy. And it never changes—ever. You see, Jonathan, that's how I managed to get you. I sought you and even your unborn seed from generations before you. Don't forget. I'm timeless. I know who has been called, and ordained, and set aside, and sanctified to do great works for him. It's just that THEY don't know. And it's my job to steal their vision, kill their faith, and destroy souls. That's my job. And believe me, it works more times than you would think. But if I can get into the vision, faith and soul of a young person, then I can destroy or at least dilute the integrity of the offspring. And then—generation by generation—I will continue to dilute each subsequent seed until there is no vision, faith or hope left. And then I'VE GOT THEM—for the next umpteen generations. I'm wicked. But I'm very organized.

JONATHAN

(Without as much as a though or glance. Pointing back toward Satan) You know what? I've only got one word for your, Satan—and that word is JESUS!! (Satan only throws up his hands and returns to a worshiping posture.) And I hope you stay that way forever!! (Goes over to the angel and shows him his report. To the angel.) He was going to destroy me and then use me to even destroy my family and even the very lineage of my seed. (To Satan) Why me, Lucifer?

SATAN

Well, John-John, you ARE the weakest link.

JONATHAN

How so, Lucifer?

SATAN

Because you never believed the word of truth, Jonathan. And those who do not believe truth is damned already. They are like fruits on the trees of an easily accessible orchid. They are like clouds without water and smart men who are fools. I pluck them at my leisure and use them to contaminate the rest of the harvest. I told you, Jon-Jon. Evil? Certain. Patient? Purposely? Organized. Even the more! Good-bye!

JONATHAN

Good bye is right you master demon! I'm leaving here. And while I'm at it, I think I'll just take this with me. (Grabs the book) Now I can warn people about you and what you're trying to do to them.

SATAN

Don't be a complete fool, Jonathan. Never will anybody hear or believe you. Who will ever believe that you've visited hell and returned? There's too much Star Wars and technology and manmade miracles around them for them to truly believe in anything as spiritual as heaven and hell. To them I'm just a fairy tale. I'm just an evil man with a long tail and a red outfit. I'm not real. I don't really exist in their minds and hearts, and because I don't, they will never fortify themselves against me. They're like ducks sitting on a pond during hunting season. Just another weak link. Smart men have become too wise to believe this truth. And unlearned men have become too doubtful to receive it. For me, Jon-Jon, the harvest truly is plenteous AND my demonic laborers are too. Your "fairy tale" will never be believed on Earth. You will be scored and mocked with laughter. You'll be ridiculed and said to be a fool. You would do better not to mention this little ordeal to your friends "back home".

JONATHAN

No! I'll tell them anyway! I'll show them this book. I'll tell them everything I saw and experienced down here today. I'll make SOMEBODY believe. If I can only get one person to believe and to not come here, that's a help. I'll tell them. I'll tell them. (Family voices can be heard praying.)

ANGEL

We are ordered to leave now. Our work here is done. Stay with me as we walk through valley of the shadow of death. But you must fear no evil. For his rod and his staff are with you to comfort and protect you.

JONATHAN

Don't worry. I'm not afraid anymore. I'm a believer . . . and a true believer doesn't have the spirit of fear.

ANGEL

This way, Jonathan.

JONATHAN

One last thing . . . please!! (Angel nods agreeably. Points to Satan and yells . . .) JESUS!!! (Satan falls to his knees and begins worshipping. Jonathan goes over and pushes Satan down to a prone position and places his foot on Satan's back. To the angel.) I just want to be able to say that for once in my life, I have really had the devil under my feet!! (Returns to the angel and they exit.)

SATAN

(Screaming hysterically) Where are you going? Where are you going? You can't leave? Not hell! Nobody leaves here! Nobody. Get back here, Jonathan! You hear me. I said get back here! No-o-o-ow!! Jonathan!! Jonathan!!

(LIGHTS)

(The family continues in a prayerful mode/posture. Kortashia peeps over at her brother and notices a slight movement of one of his hands beneath the covering sheet.)

KORTASHIA

Oh God!! OH GOD!! OH-H-H GOD!! He moved! He moved! His little finger actually moved. I saw it!

MR COLLINS

You sure, Tasshia?

KORTASHIA

Daddy, of course I'm sure. I was just opening my eyes from prayer when I . . . . You see? (Pointing) You see?

MS COLLINS

MY GOD!! She's right, Shedrick! She's right! I saw it. I saw it. Dead people don't move. Get the doctor! Get the doctor. Quick. By the power of the Holy Spirit, I declare Lazarus, you've done it again! (Kortashia rushes out of the room and returns quickly with the doctor and nurse. They enter, notice the movement, and immediately begin to perform medical procedures again. The family is huddled together closely quietly giving thanks for what has transpired. The medical team has rushed back into the OR and is again working frantically on Jonathan. A mixture of praises and medical instructions can be heard.)

LIGHTS

(A day later at the Collins' home. Once again it is dinner time. The family is around the table and the discussion is jovial.)

KORTASHIA

What I really want to know is what does it feel like to be dead, Jonathan? Is it scary?

JONATHAN

I don't think dying is scary at all. It's the living after you've died that's scary.

MR. COLLINS

You mean such as in heaven or hell, huh?

JONATHAN

Yeah, Dad, I do. It's funny because it's so easy to end up in hell and not even recognize that you're choosing hell every day of your life as your final destination.

MR. COLLINS

But we pray and thank God for his covering and protection over this family and for the spiritual truth that not one member of this household shall ever occupy as much as a foot space in the pit of hell.

JONATHAN

And I just want to thank God for a praying family.

MS. COLLINS

Amen! No hell bound souls in this house!

JONATHAN

Dad, before all of this happened to me the other day, you said we needed to take a long overdue walk and have a man to man talk.

MR. COLLINS

I did.

JONATHAN

Still think we need to have that talk?

MR. COLLINS

Jonathan, a talk between a boy and his father doesn't have to be long or overdue. It just needs to be often. Why you ask? Got something you want to tell me?

JONATHAN

You betcha! Mom, you and Kortorshia might want to hear this too. I really think you will.

KORTORSHIA

(Getting up and grabbing the family's coats and quickly handing them out to everybody.) Let's go! I've got cabin fever anyway. We can all stop for ice cream down on 14th and Forman Avenue.

JONATHAN

It's about hell. That's what I want to talk to y'all about today. Hell. (Everyone exits.)

MR. COLLINS

What about hell, son?

JOHNATHAN

Dad, it's real. It's a real place. And there's a real devil. And there are real consequences for every choice and decision we make while we are here on earth.

MS. COLLINS

Really now?

JOHNTHAN

No, Mom, seriously. The devil is real. And he even knows the word of God . . . REAL GOOD too. And what he does is he creates situations here on earth to cause you to doubt or choose against God's word so that you will end up in hell with him. It's really simple, but you just don't see it when you're doing it.

MR. COLLINS

Now do you see why it is so important that families pray and stay in the word of God together?

JOHNTHAN

Oh you better believe I do now! I didn't before, but, yes, YES, I do now. Never again will he deceive me the way he did before. Fool me once, shame on you. Fool me twice, shame on me! (Laughter) Hey, Mom, Dad, Torshia, I'm really sorry about how I acted and the things I said the other day. And, Dad, if you had taken me by that clinic the other day, I would have come up positive for drug use—marijuana and alcohol. But I promise you never again. NEVER. I have learned my lesson . . . and the deceiver will never have my soul again.

KORTORSHA

Well . . . what more is there to be said? Is everybody ready? Sorry to cut your story off Jonathan, but I'm salivating for some of that fresh ice cream right now.

MS. COLLINS

Well! I think we're about as ready as can be.

KORTORSHA

I know I am. I can't wait to get a double scoop of that black walnut and almond cheery ice cream.

JOHNTHAN

Goodness, Torshia! Two scoops? I've been all the way to hell and back and I still ain't seen nobody else as greedy as you. Why two scoops? You're just greedy!

KORTORSHA

Alright! Don't start no stuff. I ain't said nothing about how much you eat or how many scoops you're going to get. So just mind your own business big brother! Just because I prayed for you while you were in hell doesn't mean you can come back here and control my appetite! (Exiting as they speak)

JOHNTHAN

I'm just saying. Two of those giant scoops for somebody your size, now that's just plain old greedy!

KORTORSHA

Oh I see. You got short people jokes now, huh? Ain't no shame in my game. Jive all you want!

MS. COLLINS

You two children! Let's go, baby, before they drive both of us straight looney!

(Mr. Collins looks up to heaven as if offering up a quick pray. Exits.)

LIGHTS

(IN THE BLACK THE VOICE CAN BE HEARD.)

I'll be back for you again, Jonathan. And this time I will send seven demons for you instead of just one. I WILL sift you as wheat. But now I will depart for a season only to seek more about you—your strengths, your weaknesses, your temptations, your hurts and disappointments, your fears and your desires. Oh yes—I will return, Jonathan. And when I do, I will be sure to make you . . . . my next long-term house guest . . . . good bye. Ha! HA HA! HA!

CURTAINS

THE OTHER SIDE OF JORDAN

The Other Side of Jordan is set in the late 1950's. The family is poor, yet its members (minus Saul) are moralists, Christians, and family oriented. Their home is mundane. Their religious and spiritual backgrounds and beliefs are the basics of their faith. Beth, the mother, is the uneducated but staunch believing backbone and glue of the family. Her desires, intents, and efforts are to have a happy and saved family while still on this side of Jordan; however, she learns, that there are some things we just won't get on this side of Jordan, and some things we can't avoid on "The Other Side of Jordan."

Cast of Characters

Beth

Saul

Joshua

Martha

Voice of God

Mother Elque

Sister Brinson

Sister Estee

Medical attendant

Church sisters

Church members

ACT I

SCENE I

BETH:

(Mother [Beth] is frantically running back and forth between the kitchen [where she is preparing her Sunday's breakfast and dinner] and the living room [where she is energetically tidying up her home] while humming an old Negro spiritual. She is clad in her sleeping garment with rolled hair and house shoes. She glances up at the coo-coo clock and whispers to herself) Lord, its done seven o'clock already. Where in the holy world *DO* the time gets to so fast now a days. You ask me I believe it either got something to do with this here technologlogy (cannot pronounce technology) or them astronauts going way out there in space. Seem to me every time they go up there and come back here time just seem to just start passing a little bit faster and faster. (Deep breath) Well ain't no sense in me loosing the rest of the time I is got left. 'Specially wid it moving so fast now and all. Best git dem chillums up fo' the sun go running off and it be night again 'fore dey can even get up and stretch. (Yelling to the children off stage) JOSHUA! OH JOSHUA!

JOSHUA:

(Voice calling from off stage) Ma-a-am, Ma.

BETH:

Uh-uh! Now don't you start no ma-a-am Ma wid me. (coo-coo clock goes off in the background) There go Tweety Bird right on time! It's seven o'clock on

221

Sunday morning and I know I ain't got to say nuthin' else to you. You neither Martha.

MARTHA:

(Voice coming from off stage) We up, Ma. You ain't got to worry.

JOSHUA:

Or preach!

BETH:

Alright Joshua! Don't you start with yo' mouth already! Now don't you have me come in there and set you straight befo' yo' feet can even hit the floor this morning.

JOSHUA:

Yes ma'am, Ma. I was just joking though.

BETH:

(laughingly) I know you was, Baby and Mama was too. But you still got to get up out of that bed. Now I told y'all last week that we was going to have to get to church early today on account of it's a special day and there'll be so many folks there by regular church time you'd have to park a block away just to get outside standing room.

JOSHUA:

Lord have mercy. Ma, we gone be in church ALL day long today, I bet. By the time all them preachers get through talking and teaching and preaching . . . and all them old mothers of the churches have they say so . . . and all the elders and superintendents and bishops speak. Then you got sixteen choirs, fours offerings, a two—hour Sunday school, another three hour main service and then another two hours worth of eating after we done with all that church. Lord, Ma, it'll be tomorrow 'fore we get back home today!

BETH:

Don't you go fretting yo' little grease-slicked head one bit, Joshua Paul 'Cause you gonna be right there dead in the middle of all that church you talking about. Cause there's one thiag you know about me for sho', and that is that I'm gonna see to it you don't miss not one minutes' worth of God's time.

SAUL:

(Saul is Beth's husband of 17 years. He is a womanizer, a drinker, gambler, occasional drug user, hater of God and church and a known wife/child abuser. [A shoe is violently tossed out of the master bedroom. It barely misses Beth's head.] Saul speaks from offstage.) Doggone it, woman, ain't I done told you 'bout getting up stirring round here this time of day on a Sunday morning! Done told you Sunday is my rest day and you and them nappy-headed chill'ums jest keep getting up here every Sunday morning jest like y'all don't know um' still in here sleeping. Now shut up that doggone noise in this house 'fore I have to get up and come out there and shut y'all up!

BETH:

(Goes over to the bedroom door and very delicately explains) But, Saul, I just wanted the children to get up a little bit early this morning 'cause . . . (Beth is showered with magazines flung in her direction by enraged Saul. Saul enters from the bedroom. He is walking menacingly and methodically toward Beth. Beth is retreating, bumbling and stumbling as she does.)

SAUL:

Who the heck asked you for that poor sounding excuse for waking me up this time of day! (He is screaming as loudly.) Did I ask you for a doggone excuse? Did I? Huh?

BETH:

(Picking up and magazines) N-n-no, Saul. N-n-no, you didn't.

SAUL:

(Madly pitching a second shoe at his wife. By now the children are standing in the living room. They are providing their mother silent consolation.) Then why the heck you bothering to say all that crap for?! I ain't got no interest in all that MESS you talking 'bout! No crowd of dumb butt people going to sit their stupid behinds up in some stupid building all day long talking 'bout they worshipping some make believe God they can't even see.

BETH:

I know you ain't, Saul. But I just thought me and the children . . .

SAUL:

SHUT UP!!! 'Cause I ain't got no interest in *whatever* you was thinking! Where my cigarettes, anyhow? I thought I left'em on the end table on yo' side of the bed last night.

BETH:

(Very calmly and politely) There *IS* no end table on MY side of the bed, Saul. You must have left your cigarettes on the end table on the side of the bed you slept in before you came in here two hours ago.

SAUL:

(Immediately and without remorse) Yeah, that must be what I did. Hey, Beth, you should'da been there. You'da got off just watching me get it on with old fine but Lucille—just like a cowboy breaking in a stallion. Y-e-e-e-e-e-h-i-i-i-i-i. Ride'm, Saul!

MARTHA:

Was that really necessary, Daddy? (Very irritated.) Do you have to go out this house EVERY night and do your little "thing" with a different woman every time then run back in here and disrespect, disregard, defile, humiliate, and embarrass us by staggering back into your family's house and giving us a play by play report as if to say (mimicking newscaster) video tape at six!! What about *us*? (Beginning to cry. Mother is trying to comfort her. She pushes away.) Don't you have even the slightest amount of respect for us. Don't you! I'm your daughter, Daddy! Doesn't that count for anything at all to you? Don't you give even the slightest DAMN about us?!

BETH:

Martha! Don't you talk like that in this house!

MARTHA:

I'm sorry, Mama, but I just can't take it no more. All the fussing and cursing and fighting and screwing around and out of wed lock children and gambling and drugs and

BETH:

(Shocked) DRUGS???

MARTHA:

Yes, Mama, drugs! Don't you ever believe (Saul appears in the door way of the bedroom. He looks the worse for wear and is visibly angered by his daughter's outburst) that man acts like that on his own. Come on, Mama! Who're his best friends? Anthony Waters. And why did Anthony and Jill break up? Because Anthony was sleeping around, pimping teenage girls, and selling crack coca in to minors! And who else does that(pointing) hang out with? Try Frankie Pierce! Number running, dice throwing, car stealing, time serving Frankie Pierce! Anybody else? Well how about Carl Slater? The infamous hit man who's been in prison three times and is up for another sentencing soon! And the list goes on! That's who this man that I have to call my daddy considers as his friends and gives more of his time to then he does to us. (Saul is intensely focused on his daughter and begins to approach her from across stage. He stops just shy of her position. He stares her eye to eye as she accuses him of being . . .) Just look at what my daddy has become in the eyes of his own daughter: A flesh peddler! A crack cocain user! A womanizer! An unfit father! An unwedded daddy! A . . . (An intense slap is heard through the family's house. Martha is knocked back over a coffee table. Her lip is split and bleeding. Her father is standing menacingly over her. She does not cry but stares coldly and motionlessly back at him. Her mother starts to her rescue. Beth freezes in her tracks as Saul's eyes and finger points her to a position on the floor.)

BETH:

(Hands up to her face. Then reaching for her daughter from across the room) Baby . . . ? (As if to ask if she's ok.)

JOSHUA:

What the heck is your problem, Dad? You sick or something? You could have killed her hitting her like that! You're evil, man. Pure evil. (He goes over to help his sister. He bends over to help his sister up but catches a knee in his face for his trouble. He falls back next to his sister, blood streaming from his noise. He too stares at his father with contempt.)

BETH:

(Nervous and unsure whether or not to come to the aid of the children. She is obviously afraid of her husband.) S-s-saul I need to help my children. (He stares at her menacingly. He forbids her to move without ever speaking) For God's sake, Saul, my children are bleeding.

SAUL:

(Taking two steps in her direction with his fist set to deliver a blow. Beth recoils in fear. Saul stops then announces . . .)SHUT UP. WOMAN!! UHM THE MAN IN DIS HOUSE! YOU JUST DO WHAT I TELL YOU TO WHEN I TELL YOU TO AND OTHER THAN THAT YOU JUST KEEP YO' DAMN MOUTH CLOSED 'LESS I SAY SO!! (Returns to the kids who are still on the floor.) Lil' girl, don't you NEVER again long as you live call me none of them names you just called me a minute ago. Or I swear to ALMIGHTY God I'll try my best to snatch yo pure tongue out of yo' head. You hear me? (She stares but does not answer. He kicks her leg out of the way and steps across her to address Joshua.) And if you ever defy me in my house again, boy, I'll . . . whew!! I'll tell you what. I ain't even gonna bother to tell you what I'll do to you. How 'bout that? But one thangs' for darn sure; if I was you and I was going to do some dumb stuff like that I'd do it in the summer just to be sure my friends at school wouldn't have to see what I look like after I had done it. I make myself clear, boy?

JOSHUA:

You're clear, Daddy. Real clear.

SAUL:

(Lightly slapping Joshua's face) That's good, Josh. I likes it right much when thangs is REAL clear between people. (Glances back at Martha who continues to stare) Huh! (As if nothing has happened Saul's demeanor changes instantly. He goes towards the table) Beth . . . what's for breakfast? (Beth runs over to attend to her kids. They embrace one another. Saul seats himself at the end of the table) Grits and eggs? Any that lean bacon still in the refrigerator? What about juice? I got a taste for some cold apple juice. And by the way, for all y'all church going SAINTS, I done decided no church going for y'all today.

BETH:

(In a very worried tone) Saul, what is you talking bout? Now you ain't gone start yo' regular Sunday morning shenanigans again t'day, is you? I mean after all I done told you a month of Sundays ago bout t'day being our big anniversary and all. Why, saints from everywhere gone be at Zion Grove Chaple t'day to help us praise the Lord and celebrate our anniver . . .

SAUL:

(Powerfully angry) Damn it, woman! If I done told you one time I done told you one thousand times don't you never talk to me 'bout no church, no pastor, no anniversary, no saints and above all about no something sitting way up in the sky somewhere you call a God. 'Cause if any of them was worth a DAMN why do they let this happen to you (back slaps BETH to one knee. Both kids jump up and run over to protect/console Beth.) I'm god, Beth! I'm god! And this (pointing around the house) is the world I created and these (pointing to the children) are my Adam and Eve. This is my Garden of Eden, woman! I'm God, Beth! I'm God! And before me there shall be no other. You will have no other God before me! I am alpha and omega! I'm god, Beth! (Emphatically) I AM YO' GOD, WOMAN! And I'm his god and her god too! Now get up off your lazy butt and go cook me some grits and eggs and fry me up a few big pieces of that lean bacon like you know I like it. Big pieces, Beth. You know I love me some bacon. Now git over dere and start cooking like I jest told you to woman. Git!! Git on.

BETH:

(Kids help Beth to her feet. Very calmly she reminds her husband . . .) Saul.

SAUL:

What you want with me, Beth?

BETH:

Don't forget. One day even yo' world is gonna pass away too. Where you gone live then? Y'all come on children. Y'all can help me out in the kitchen. (exit R)

SAUL:

(In a very proud and self satisfying voice and laughing to himself) I like that! That's alright! At least they know who God is now. (Starts off l then stops and yells back over his r shoulder) And don't be too long. I ain't had nothing to eat since I ate that chicken over at Lucille's house last night. (exits)

ACT I

SCENE II

(The family [minus Saul] is sitting around the kitchen table after breakfast. Both kids display visual abuse marks)

MARATHA:

Why, Mama? Why?

BETH:

Why what, Baby?

SAUL:

You know what she's asking, Mama.

BETH:

Yeah. I know what she means. And I'm not sure I can make her understand why I stay with yo' Daddy. I know I could leave and make do with what little help we could git from friends, family and the church. Dunno. Government might even decide to give us a lil' help too. Add that to what little bit of money I makes washing and cleaning for folks, we could probably do just as well for ourselves I reckon. But I can't go nowhere. You see, I promised the Lord and vowed to that man that I would be here with him for better or for worse, for richer or for poorer, in sickness and in health for as long as I shall live.

MARTHA:

But, Mama, this ain't the same man you made them vows with. You never vowed to stay with no abusive drug addict. You never vowed to stay with no wife beating husband. (Joshua moves away from the table and over to the refrig.) You never vowed to stay with no promiscuous man or no child abuser.

JOSHUA:

And what about HIM, Mama? What did he vow? (Open refrigerator door. Interior is nearly bare) Did he vow to feed us? Well he reneged. (Goes over and collects a stack of bills. Brings them back to the table, opens them and reads them aloud to his mother one at a time.) Electric bill. Total due $114 with a final reminder enclosed. Water bill $16 with a termination of services notices enclosed. Rent—should I even bother to say? Electric services scheduled for immediate disconnection unless you pay at least $45 of the existing $60 balance. Do I need to read more of our gloom and doom financial affairs, Mama? (Throws the remainder of the bills in the center of the table) What's my point? My point is did he vow to head this household and assume the responsibilities of a *father, husband and man*? If he did he either reneged on his vows or he was straight out lying when he made them. Now I don't know about you or Martha but I've had just about all of this I can take. I just ain't fit to take no more busted noses and hell raising sessions unless I can raise hell and fight back too.

BETH:

Now, Joshua, you just sit down there and listen to what I got to tell you.

JOSHUA:

No, Mama. Not anymore. Never again.

BETH:

What are you talking about? What are you saying? (Very perplexed) You sit down, Joshua.

JOSHUA:

No, Mama. (Sadly) I don't have time. I've got to go.

BETH:

Go? Joshua what on earth are you talking about . . . go? What's got into you dis morning? Now I realize we all be a little upset 'bout what went on in here this morning, but . . .

JOSHUA:

No, Mama. No. You really don't realize. And it ain't all about this morning either. You see, Ma, I ain't never made no vows to stay with nobody who was going to beat up on me, and disrespect me, and disown me, and keep me shut up in a small house like animals locked up in a cage. I ain't never took no vows before God or nobody else that said I would stay with a drug user, a pimp, a gambler, a liar, a thief, an a woman's—any woman's—man, and a down right human dog till death US do part. Now maybe *you* did. And if you did then you do that. But as for me . . . I'm gonna have to write y'all and call y'all so that I can let y'all know how I'm doing.

BETH:

How you doing? Lord, child, wait a minute. Just sit down. (Rubbing her head and going over to coax Joshua into sitting at the table.) Now, Josh, you jest hold on a minute now. Son, I knows it gets powerfully hard for you and yo' sister to put up with a lot dat go on 'round here sometime. But it gets just as hard for me too. And without y'all and the Lord I just don't know if I could make it neither, Son. (Joshua pushes away and walks across stage. He sits on the couch. Beth trails him and continues to make her point) Josh . . . (taking his hand) you and Martha's all I got . . . that really mean anything to me, that is. I live like I do as much for y'all as I do for myself and the Lord. I sacrifice so y'all can have. I cry at night so y'all can smile during the day. My belly's many times empty and growling jest so y'all's don't have to be. (Martha comes over and consoles her mother.)

MARTHA:

Mama, we know that. And God knows we 'prechiate it too. But Josh is right, Mama. This is getting old. I get whipped up on now more than I did when I was little. I'm tired of going to school every Monday lying to my friends and teachers about a different bruise, scratch or scar my drunk daddy done put on me. I'm tired of being laughed at by my friends because they saw my daddy bumbling drunk in the streets somewhere. I'm tired of shiftless old men putting their hands all over me because they've seen my daddy put his hands all over other young girls my age. I'm tired of failing in classes I should be passing because of what's going on in this house.

BETH:

But . . . But . . . Baby.

MARTHA:

No! Mama no! Just try to listen to me and understand what I feel just one time, Mama. Listen, Mama, Joshua is right and you know it. But you just won't admit it 'cause you feel that if you stay here with that drunken, child molesting, despicable creature (voice escalating) . . . as you have for nearly twenty whole years of your life . . . the best twenty years of your life I might add . . . you think somehow . . . miraculously you will wake up one day and that big sorry sack of . . . (notices the look on mom's face) well you know what I would like to call him . . . anyway—you think he will have magically changed? Well, Mama, it hasn't happened in all these years. It's not happening as we speak! And if we predicted the future on the basis of the past, then it's safe to say (pointing toward the bedroom door) he who sleeps as human manure will certainly awaken as manure. (Until now Martha has not noticed her father who is standing in the doorway of his bedroom holding the breakfast plate from which he has eaten his a.m. meal. There is a brief stare between the two, however she shows no fear. Pause. Then with eyes still meeting dad's . . .) Joshua's right, Ma. I'm tired. I can't take no more of this either. I'm leaving too.

BETH:

LEAVING?!?!

SAUL:

Leaving? What the hell is you talking girl? Huh? What is you talking about some leaving for?

MARTHA:

(Obviously ignoring her father and going over and speaking directly to BETH) You see, Ma, me and Josh, we called around last week and asked for help. We knew you'd never leave here but we figured we'd better while we still could. So the folks down at the Child Advocacy Office told us that if any more disturbances came up that we felt we couldn't deal with just call them and they'd come pick us up or we could walk to the nearest shelter. Well, Ma, it's time to walk.

SAUL:

Walk? Walk? Walk? You fool!!! You think I'm just gone stand here like Lil' Johnny Fresh Off The Turnip Truck and just let you WALK out of this house? (There's a brief quiet pause of anticipation.) You want to walk? You want to walk. Ok you just be there when I get back and I'll make sure you walk. All of y'all! Y'all want to walk. OK doggone it (voice becoming very excited) then walk y'all will! (Throws down plate and glass and exits to his bedroom)

MARTHA:

Oh no, Mama, he's going to get the gun again. Please Mama stop him!

JOSHUA:

Quick, Martha get over there behind the couch. (Martha stands in the doorway to prevent Saul access to the family. A physical struggle ensues.)

BETH:

SAUL!! SAUL NO!! SAUL PLEASE! NO SAUL! PLEASE NO! NOT THE GUN! SAUL PLEASE DON'T HURT US! SAUL PLEASE NOT MY CHILDREN! NO SAUL! NO-O-O-O!! (Martha is backhanded across the face and slung onto the living room floor. Joshua places himself between his sister and the gun. His mother is too far away for him to shield her from the father.)

SAUL:

(Goes over and places the gun on the tip of his son's nose) So y'all feel like walking this morning, huh? Y'all feel like walking down to the Child Advocacy Office and reporting me to the authorities, huh? Now do you think your old daddy is stupid enough to let y'all do something like that?

BETH:

(Slowly getting to her feet) Saul please. They're just children. Don't do this to them. Think about what you're doing, Saul. Look at the fear on their faces. Can't you see their hearts beating? For God's sake, Saul, can you see what you're doing to all of us . . . even yourself? Saul . . .

SAUL:

(Abruptly turns and points the pistol at his wife's head) I THOUGHT I TOLD YOU TO SHUT YOUR MOUTH WOMAN!!! NOW DO I HAVE TO SAY IT AGAIN OR DO I HAVE TO TAKE IT OUT (stops suddenly and smiles. voice declined he finishes his question)—on Adam or Eve.

Adam! Adam! Where art thou, Adam. Have you been eating from my tree of life again, Adam? And you, Eve? Have you been talking to your little serpent friend again? Be careful with him, Eve. I heard rumors he comes from a bad neighborhood. Adam! Come out and talk to me. It's me Adam. God! Creator of all! (cough, cough). King of Kings and (cough, cough) Lord of Lords. Adam where art thou? (To his wife) You see, (cough) I told you fools I am God! Worship me my servants! (Brandishes the pistol as he speaks.) Worship me I say! (They all bow repeatedly on hands and knees as if worshipping Saul.) Yes worship me my servants! Worship me! (Cough, cough) FOR I AM GOD! I AM GOD! (Cough)AND BESIDE ME THERE IS NO OTHER! I AM GOD! (CURTAINS close with Saul angrily brandishing his pistol skyward and his dominion over his family. The family is bowing to Saul.)

ACT II

SCENE I

(Act II Scene I takes place in the family's home. It is the following Monday. Ruth is clothed appropriately to receive guests but she wears sunglasses to hide the effects of her abuse. She is visited by two of her fellow church members who are discussing with her the events and success of yesterday's anniversary. It is obvious they know of the abusive history of this family and hold no particular liking for Saul. When the curtain opens Beth is again cleaning her home. From off stage she is interrupted by the doorbell. Then a second time and quickly thereafter a third ring.)

BETH:

Hee-e-ey!!! I heard you! I heard you! Just give me a minute and I'll get there. (Taking off her apron and laying it across the back of a nearby chair.) Lord these chillums is always in a hurry now a day. Can't wait on nothing no mo'. Lord knows they want everything right now and right here. (Prepares to open the door then remembers to put on her sunglasses first. Door bell rings again.) Hey!! I said I was coming, didn't I? Now what y'all chilluns . . . (Notices who it is) Lord, lord, lord!!! Just look at who the wind done blown by MY house. Lord, sisters, Why y'all just better come right on in here and proceed to sit down and make yo'selves just as comfortable as y'all want to be. Praise the Lord, it sure is good to see y'all. (Two sisters and an older mother of the church enter the house.)

MOTHER ELQUE:

Sister Anderson we can't stay long at all, darling. We were just out visiting the sick and shut in and decided to drop in because we just figured you had to be some awfully sick for you to miss the big anniversary yesterday.

BETH:

(Searching for words, but trying desperately not to lie to the mother) Well, mother you might say I started out doing just fine first thing yesterday morning but in just a little while—nad I mean it didn't take long a bit either—something just hit me and knocked me right off my feet.

SISTER ESTEE:

(A no nonesense sister who obviously speaks her mind, which is why she often travels around with the more refined Mother Elque.) That SOMETHING wasn't named Saul (peeking beneath Beth's sunglasses) by chance was it now?

BETH:

(Repositioning sunglasses and ignoring the question) A-a—and you might say I just couldn't get back up on my feet right after it hit me.

SISTER ESTEE:

Huh! I know that's right. 'Cause most of the time you usually can't.

SISTER BRINSON:

Sister Anderson, how are the children?

BETH:

Oh they're doing just fine. Joshua went down the street visiting and Lil' Martha, she . . .

SISTER BRINSON:

(Very stern) Sister Anderson! (Deep breath and pause. She leans over and gently touches Beth's cheeks then slowly and gingerly removes the sunglasses. Beth offers no resistance. Beth is embarrassed of her visible scars.) Sister this isn't the first or second or third or fourth time he's done this you know. And personally I feel like Saul beating up on you simply done got old now Sister Anderson. And every time he does it to you he does the same thing to the children too. So why don't you tell me now. (Very motherly) How are the children?

BETH:

Sister Brinson (starting very tentatively) they be alright. Martha, well he kinda busted up her nose a little bit and Joshua . . . well . . . (deep breath)well his mouth will heal in a little or no time at all. Like I done said, my chillums they be alright.

MOTHER ELQUE:

So what you're telling us, Sister Anderson is that he beat the children again too.

BETH:

(Dejectedly) Yes'am. I reckon I am telling you that—again! (Turns and starts across stage. Swirls around with tears welling in her eyes) But Mother Elque it's gonna stop. I just know it is! He ain't gonna stay like this all his life. I mean what sane man can just keep beating up on a good wife and two loving children ALL his life for no reason?

SISTER ESTEE:

What SANE man you know would spend *any part* of his life beating up on a good wife and loving children for no reason, Sister?

BETH:

But Sister Estee!! It ain't like Saul is insane or nothing like that.

MOTHER ELQUE:

Then what is it like, Sister Anderson?

BETH:

Well . . . (having a hard time coming up with words) Well . . . . Well . . .

MOTHER ELQUE:

There must be more to this description than just WELL, Sister Anderson.

BETH:

Mother Elque, look. I know what I mean . . .

SISTER BRINSON:

Then TELL us, Sister, so we'll know what you mean as "well."

BETH:

I guess I just can't explain it so good to nobody else. Mother—Sisters listen to me (Enter Joshua and Martha. The sisters extend their arms and greet the children with a hug and friendly kiss. They too are wearing sunglasses. The sisters remove their glasses and examine their bruises. Beth is now singing a church hymn.)

MOTHER ELQUE:

I've heard what you've said, Sister Anderson. But I've also just examined the bruises on your children's faces. And when I touched them the hands of my spirit felt the bruises on their souls. Their spirits are being tortured. Their dignity is being compromised. Their self esteemed is being undermined. Their minds are confused and cluttered and their hope is fleeing as we speak. And while you're living for the day when GOD's gonna change this situation for *you* your children are dying—NOW!

BETH:

Mother Elque, what are you saying?

SISTER ESTEE:

(Extremely feisty) Honey she's saying be a saint ALWAYS—but a fool NEVER. Now you look-a-here, Sister. Enough of anything is enough. And while God gave you faith, He also gave you common sense too. DIDN'T HE? If he didn't you better come on down to the church and get in the prayer line and get yourself some.

MOTHER ELQUE:

Sister Anderson, God knows your heart. All you got to do is fall on your knees and pray to him in faith and truth and in his own way and in his own time He will deliver you from the hands of your wicked oppressor. Sister Anderson always remember this. (MUSICAL SELECTION TBA. Mother and sisters. Following selection . . .) Now sister it's time for us to leave. We came by only to check on your condition and to spread a word of compassion your way. Remember, Sister, you are the steward not only for your spirit, but their (pointing to the children) spirits too. Just think about it, okay? For the children—think about it. Can we pray before we leave, Sister? (She extends her hands and the cast joins hands in a circular fashion center stage.) Father in the Holy name of Jesus Christ your son, we come before you today with humbled spirits and receptive hearts requesting the wisdom and guidance of your divine spirit. We come before you asking for mercy and compassion in the lives of these people your servants. We come (Saul enters the front door, slams it behind him and stands and stares menacingly at the group. Mother Elque peeps through one eye and sees it's Saul then hurriedly concludes her prayer.) and now we see it time for us to go. And all that agreed with that prayer said . . .

ALL:

Amen.

SAUL:

(Coughing more noticeably now, Saul speaks to his wife in a highly threatening voice as he Approaches her.) Ain't I done told you enough times now that I don't want none of these here sanctified Christian freaks in my house! How come you think I wouldn't let you go to church yesterday? 'Cause I done decided you don't need none of these holy fools and none of that holy ghost foolishness in my house! Ain't I done told you that already? Ain't I?

SISTER ESTEE:

(Taking off her hat and rolling up her sleeves) Now you just ho-o-o-l-ld it right there, Saul Anderson!! Now just who you think you're calling a holy fool?

MOTHER ELQUE:

Sister Estee, please, don't forget who and what you are.

SISTER ESTEE:

I know who and what I am alright, Mother. And just as soon as I take my salvation off and lay it over here on the arm of this chair, I also know who and what I'm just about ready to become up in this house too. (Still rolling up her sleeves. Turns and speaks to Saul.) Now I know you don't want me to have to take off my God's glory and lay it over there on that chair while I deal with you outside of the Holy Spirit.

SAUL:

(Firing back at Sister Estee) Shut up woman! You sanctified fool! (To Beth) If you'da done like I told you in the first place these darn hoodlums wouldn't even be in my house anyway. But you didn't, did you? (pointing to and slowly approaching Beth as she backs away cross stage.) I told you yesterday I was yo' God. DIDN'T I?

MARTHA:

(As if in a daze and disbelief that this could be happening again) Daddy no please. Don't do this again. Please don't.

SAUL:

(As if he never heard his daughter speak) I made you bow down on the Sabbath and worship me. DIDN'T I?!?

MARTHA:

S-s-s-aul. Please, Saul, don't do us like this in front of folks. Saul please.

MARTHA:

Daddy no. Please don't make me see you like this *all* the time. Daddy . . .

SAUL:

And now today I come back to my Garden of Eden and I find you keeping company with Lucifer *her*self and *her* follies! Well, maybe I just need to show yo' friends—hell's angels—just how I go about keeping law and order in my universe. (Saul pushes her back over the arm of the couch. She falls then rolls onto the floor.)

MARTHA:

(Still standing frozen in place) Daddy, all we want to do is love you. Why do you keep doing this to us?

JOSHUA:

(Runs over and stands between Mom and Dad. Begins to plea) Dad, no. Not again. We-We just can't take this again. Please Dad. Just leave her alone. She didn't mean any harm.

SAUL:

MOVE (a hard slap is delivered at the same time as the word move is spoken) outta my way, Boy!! I've got a lesson to teach this here Christian mama of yours! (Standing over BETH bellowing) Get up! GET UP I SAID. I ain't done with you yet! Get up woman so I can show these sanctified fools how yo' God runs his universe! GET UP I SAY!!

MOTHER ELQUE:

(Steps between the couple) Mr. Anderson please don't do this to her. We'll leave now if that will make you happy, but she certainly doesn't deserve . . . (he pushes the mother back over an end table and onto the floor. Lightening-like Sister Estee rushes over and lands a straight right followed by a left-right combination then firmly kicks Saul in the groins. He curls up in pain and, bowed together, falls to the floor groaning. She straddles his upper chest and quickly delivers a few more firm blows to his face before Mother Elque's voice stops further punching.)

MOTHER ELQUE:

S-I-S-T-E-R!!!!! NO! NO SISTER!! LET HIM GO! Let . . . him . . . go, Sister Estee.

SISTER ESTEE:

GO?! GO?!

MOTHER ELQUE:

(Very calmly) Go. Let him go, Sister.

SISTER ESTEE:

After I done took my salvation off and done put it (Looking around as if looking for her religion)—somewhere 'round here—you want me to just let him go? The only thing I'm thinking about letting go right now is another right hook straight 'cross his head!

MOTHER ELQUE:

Sister Estee, no matter the situation you must remember to never permit yourself to be overcome by anger.

SISTER ESTEE:

(Breathing deeply and staring down at Saul who is still appearing somewhat shocked by the events. Sister Estee's tone clearly defies her comment.) I ain't angry, Mother.

MOTHER ELQUE:

Good. Good. That's very good, Sister.

SISTER ESTEE:

Well, then, can I beat him up 'cause I'm happy. (Faking a smile at Saul)

MOTHER ELQUE:

Sister! Of course not! We must always remember who we are, Sister . . . and conduct ourselves accordingly.

SISTER ESTEE:

Oh I remember who I am alright. I'm George Foreman's second cousin one time removed. And if you'd just let me throw just one more right hook to this boy's head, I'll show you—and HIM—just how accordingly I really can act.

MOTHER ELQUE:

Sister we will not fight and that's final. You will let Saul up off the floor now.

SISTER BRINSON:

(To Beth) Sister do you think it's safe for us to leave now? I mean we shouldn't stay here too much longer and wear out our welcome of course . . . (interrupted by Sister Estee still sitting straddled Saul's chest).

SISTER ESTEE:

(Peering down at Saul with her fist recoiled.) We can stay here just as lon-n-ng as we wants to. Now can't we, Saul?

MOTHER ELQUE:

Sister Brinson is right I'm afraid. I'm sure it would be better if we left. (To the family) But y'all can come with us if you think that would be in your best interest.

SAUL:

They ain't going nowhere I tell you! NO where! Not lessen I done said so. And I ain't said neither one of them can go nowhere you none of you bunch of hell's angels. (Couch. Sister Estee recoils her fist and Saul cringes in anticipation. She is still sitting on his chest.)

BETH:

Mother, we'll be alright. Don't worry. I'm tired of running now. I'm tired of bruises . . . and I'm tired of living in fear. Me and my children done took all the beatings we gonna ever take. The Lord done showed me that it's all in his hands now. We done done all we can. We done prayed . . . and cried . . . and hoped . . . and forgave. But the Lord says revenge is His. He gonna set this record straight Himself. You just can't keep knocking God's own children around and think their father ain't gonna have no say so in the matter sooner or later. You gonna be sorry, Saul. But the Lord says *this* done gone on long enough. (Walks over and points down to Saul) That was yo' last free shot. Lord knows I hope it was best one—cause you in deep trouble from here on in. Saul (pause) I ain't running from you never again—never no mo'.

SISTER BRINSON:

Well, sisters, I think our work here is done. (Looks at her watch then shows it to Saul as if he's interested) Lord just look at how the time done got away from here. Mother, we better be getting about our way. (Saul coughs)

MOTHER ELQUE:

Josh would you like to come with us to visit the sick and shut in?

JOSHUA:

Sure, Mother. It'll do me good. I'll wait outside near the car. (To his mother) You gonna be alright? (She smiles and nods yes and kisses him on the cheek. He exits center stage.)

MOTHER ELQUE:

And you Martha?

MARTHA:

(Drops her head in obvious disgust.) No. I'm going to my room to lie down and think for a while, but I can't promise you that I'll be alright. I just can't promise that anymore. (Exits)

MOTHER ELQUE:

I'm sorry all of this had to happen again today, Sister. This was not our intent.

BETH:

I know, Mother.

MOTHER ELQUE:

Be faithful and prayerful, daughter, and we will see you in church on Sunday.

SISTER ESTEE:

(Finally getting up off Saul's chest) Yeah—and be SURE you bring THIS sorry thang with'cha. Lord knows he needs some serious prayer!

MOTHER ELQUE:

SISTER!!! (Admonishingly. Then to Beth) Call us if you need anything at all. (Cutting her eyes back at Saul) And I do mean anything too.

BETH:

I will, Mother.

SISTER ESTEE:

(Glaring back at Saul rolling her sleeves down.) Sister, you remember now—EN-NE-THANG!! AT ALL!! Huh? EN-NE-THANG!! (Saul glares back and coughs. THEY EXIT.)

(THERE IS SILENCE ON STAGE. BOTH CHARACTERS MOVE ABOUT THE STAGE AS IF AVOIDING ONE ANOTHER. ENTER MARTHA AND STANDS UPSTAGE OBSERVING THE UNUSUAL BEHAVIOR. FINALLY SAUL THROWS DOWN THE MAGAZINE HE IS HOLDING AND RUSHES UP TO BETH. HE GRABS HER IN HER COLLAR AND DRAWS BACK HIS HAND AS IF HE IS PREPARING TO SLAP HER. SHE STARES HIM SQUARELY IN HIS EYES BUT DOES NOT MOVE OR FLINCH. HE FEINTS A BLOW, THEN A SECOND ONE. SHE DOES NOT MOVE. SHE IS STARING DEEP INTO HIS EYES. THERE IS NO FEAR IN HER FOR THE FIRST TIME IN HER MARRIED LIFE. THE POSE IS HELD FOR ABOUT 10 SECONDS. SAUL RELEASES HER COLLAR AND ATTEMPTS TO SHOVE HER BACK BUT SURPRISINGLY SHE DOES NOT MOVE. BETH RELEASES HER STARE AND STEPS AWAY FROM HIM. HE IS OBVIOUSLY

SHOCKED AND OUTDONE. SPEECHLESS, HE STARTS TOWARDS THE BEDROOM THEN STOPS.)

SAUL:

This ain't over yet woman. You'll see. 'Fore long I've have you right back just the way you wuz before them holy sister friends of yours stopped in here. (cough)

BETH:

No Saul. It's over. It's all over. The beatings . . . the fear . . . the intimidation . . . the bruises . . . the scars . . . . They all over, Saul. All over.

SAUL:

Not yet, Baby. Not yet. It ain't over 'till I—yo' *GOD*—say it's over.

BETH:

My God did say it's over, Saul. He just did. That's why I'm telling you. God done told me to tell you. You done already been whipped with stripes that you ain't even got enough sense to know they done struck you. But it's over. Your sins done found you out, Saul. Yo' wages ain't long from being paid. You better listen to this *sanctified fool*, MAN, and hear what God done said about you. (Saul is staring but saying nothing.) God's got it all in His hand and only He can forgive you now. By the way, Saul, that cough you got, if I was you, I'd go get it checked out—QUICK—'cause your world is about to start crumbling—real soon now. Real soon. And then Saul, where you gonna run to? Where you spend your eternity, Saul? Where? Where are you gonna spend eternity after yo lil' kingdom done fell apart—(mockingly)god? (Saul turns and walks off stage. Coughs. Beth begins humming an old church hymn. Martha rushes to her mother {center stage} and embraces her. Martha continues singing.

LIGHTS

ACT II

SCENE II

(Scene II takes place the following Sunday at church. The action opens with the congregation concluding the old hymn "Till We Meet Again." Following the song the congregation stands for the benediction which is delivered by Rev. Flount.)

REVERN:

May the words of my mouth

CONGREGATION:

May the words of my mouth

REVERN:

And the meditation of my heart

CONGREGATION:

And the meditation of my heart

REVERN:

Be acceptable in thy sight

CONGREGATION:

Be acceptable in thy sight

REVERN:

Oh, Lord, my strength and my redeemer

CONGREGATION:

Oh, Lord, my strength and my redeemer

REVERN:

In Jesus name we pray

CONGREGATION:

In Jesus name we pray

REVERN:

And the church said

ALL:

Amen. (Congregants began to greet one another as they exit the church. Ruth is suddenly noticed by Mother Elque and is greeted

with a big hug and encouraging smile.)

MOTHER ELQUE:

God bless you, Sister Anderson. How are you today? Wasn't service just glorious this morning? And didn't the pastor deliver a message straight out of heaven? (Appears more excited than her previous demeanor.)

BETH:

Good morning and God bless you too, Mother. (Smiling) I'm fine and yes . . . yes . . . and yes. (They laugh)

JOSHUA:

Good morning, Mother.

MOTHER ELQUE:

Good morning, Joshua. Oh Sister Anderson you would have been so proud of him last week. Why he was simply magnificent during our sick and shut in visits.

BETH:

Why thank you, Mother. (Sisters Brinson and Estee approach from across the church and interrupt Beth's speech with a big hug.) I'm very proud of him even though there be times I do wonder just where DO that boy finds the strength . . . I mean seeing how his daddy is and all . . . you know. It ain't like he got no man to look up to or nothing. (deep breath) But somehow . . . somehow . . . he just keep right on making me and the Lord awfully proud of him.

SISTER ESTEE:

I know what you mean, Sister. It's so sad that a lot of us married women is married only in the bed. Outside of the bed and away from the kitchen table we be hard pressed to even see them low down thangs we call our husbands.

MOTHER ELQUE:

SISTER ESTEE!! Why I . . .

SISTER ESTEE:

(Quickly interrupting the mother and pointing her finger skyward) Don't you tell that lie! Don't you do it. Don't you say you ain't never. Cause I KNOW you have. Now don't start acting like Sister Anderson the only one up in here that done messed up and married a two legged dog. (Louder) I know better'n dat! Y'all remember that old saying—if you lay down with dogs you'll get up with flees.

ALL:

Yeah sure.

SISTER ESTEE:

Well not to call no names but I done picked a whole lot of flees off people sitting in these pews many a Sunday morning. Unless'n . . . (stops, covers her mouth and looks around slowly) THEY was the dog they ownself. Lordy be, I ain't never thought of it that way. (They all erupt in laughter)

SISTER BRINSON:

Lord, sister, I just find myself in stitches every time I'm anywhere near you. God bless yo' soul!

JOSHUA:

Mama, I saw Hakeem Thompson a minute ago. When you're ready just call me I'll be outside talking to him. (Joshua turns to exit. He gets near the door when . . .)

MOTHER ELQUE:

(very stern and abrupt) Joshua!

JOSHUA:

(Stops suddenly, turns and looks as if surprised) Ma'am?

MOTHER ELQUE:

No matter what happens in your life always (counting on her fingers) trust God, take a stand, and to your own self be true. (There is silence. Joshua appears perplexed. Then . . .)

JOSHUA:

Yes ma'am, Mother. I will. (counting on his fingers.) Trust God. Take a stand. And to my own self be true. (Turns and exits)

SISTER ESTEE:

Y'all know it just don't seem right that GOOD young men like young Joshua there try so hard to become good men and the very men who fights so hard to tear them down is their own daddies.

BETH:

Yeah. You right Sister. I wish it wasn't so. But you right.

SISTER ESTEE:

But you tell little Josh to just keep holding on. 'Cause I can feel it deep down in my bones and I know he ain't gonna have to put up with this too much longer.

BETH:

Whadda ya mean, Sister Estee.

SISTER ESTEE:

It ain't for me to say, Sister. Truth is I don't know and I done said all I do know to be true. Now I don't get to feeling like this everyday. And this ain't no usual feeling for me. The last time I felt like this my little Amy passed away in her sleep. Perfectly healthy and just 17 years old too. This ain't no joke. I done seen it and like I said I kin feel it wa-a-a-ay deep in my bones. And that there boy ain't go have to fight this struggle too much longer. (Emphatically to Beth) And you ain't either! God done already took care of this battle in glory.

SISTER BRINSON:

That was real good advise you gave Joshua just a minute ago, Mother. But what was it all about. I mean, why did you even say that to him?

MOTHER ELQUE:

(Standing still and starring. Has not moved since Joshua exited.) I don't know. I just felt . . .

SISTER ESTEE:

Moved?

MOTHER ELQUE:

Yes. Yes. *Moved* to say that to him. At the right time it will all make perfectly good sense to him I'm sure.

SISTER BRIAN:

(Obviously trying to perk up the sullen moment) Well ladies WHAT did y'all cook for dinner today?

SISTER ESTEE:

Well, honey, I didn't put but two pots on the stove this morning . . . a big pot and a little pot.

BETH:

Well all I want to know is what's in the big one?

SISTER ESTEE:

Water! (laughter)

BETH:

Well Sister Estee what's in the little one then?

SISTER ESTEE:

Nothing. I just put it on the stove IN CASE

SISTER BRIAN:

In case what sister?

SISTER ESTEE:

In case I need to have something I can pick up real quick and crack Henry in the head just as soon as he starts to acting like a fool. Y'all know just how men folks can act some times. (More laughter. The laughter fades as all the sisters notice the seriousness of the mother's mood) Mother Elque, are you alright? (The mother is standing with her back to the ladies and does not answer nor move.)

BETH:

Mother?

SISTER BRINSON:

Mother Elque . . . are you alright?

MOTHER ELQUE:

(She turns slowly and looks at them. Then directly to Beth. There is a tremendous change in the Mother's voice after the first four words and as she quotes Psalms 51:1-5) The Lord God sayest . . . WHY BOASTEST THOU THYSELF IN MISCHIEF, O MIGHTY MAN? THE GOODNESS OF GOD ENDURETH CONTINUALLY. THY TONGUE DEVISETH MISCHIEFS; LIKE A SHARP RAZOR, WORKING DECEITFULLY. THOU LOVEST EVIL MORE THAN GOOD. AND LYING RATHER THAN TO SPEAK RIGHTEOUSNESS. THOU LOVEST ALL DEVOURING WORDS. O THOU DECEITFUL TONGUE. GOD SHALL LIKEWISE DESTROY THEE FOREVER, HE SHALL TAKE THEE AWAY AND PLUCK THEE OUT OF THY DWELLING PLACE AND ROOT THEE OUT OF THE LAND OF THE LIVING. FOR SUCH ARE THE REWARDS OF THE MAN WHO HAS NOT MADE GOD HIS STRENGTH.

BETH:

I have heard your prophecy, Mother. And I am confused because I don't want it to be true. What should I do, Mother? What can I expect?

MOTHER ELQUE:

You are to do nothing but wait. You are to expect nothing more than for God to keep his word, Sister Anderson. The prophesy was nothing more than your fore warning. Prepare yourself, Sister. For as the prophesy stated "For such are the rewards of the man who has not made God his strength." Sister Anderson, God's word is not for negotiation.

BETH:

B-B-But my children. (appears very worried and frightened.)

MOTHER ELQUE:

(The mother's voice has changed again.) CALL UPON ME IN THE DAY OF TROUBLE: AND I WILL DELIVER THEE,

BETH:

What about me?

MOTHER ELQUE:

CALL UPON ME IN THE DAY OF TROUBLE AND I WILL DELIVER THEE.

BETH:

(Very tearful and frightened to ask) Lord, what about Saul?

MOTHER ELQUE:

NOW CONSIDER THIS, YE THAT FORGET GOD LEST I TEAR YOU IN PIECES AND THERE WILL BE NONE TO DELIVER.

BETH:

(Bursts into tears.) Oh, Saul no! No! NO! (crying harder) All of these years I've begged and pleaded with you to straighten your life up and to do better. And now this. No! God! Please! Don't take him! (Sisters are trying to console her. She's hysterical) Please God! I know he ain't no good. I know he beats me and the children. I know he curses you, Lord. I know he won't let us go to church half the time. But, Lord, he's the only husband I got and the only daddy my children got. (Runs and kneels at the alter) Lord, please. I know this prophesy is got to come true. (Mother Elque looks heavenly. She appears to wipe a tear from her eye and is singing softly. Beth's pleas can still be heard over her singing.) But,Lord, can't You wait for just a little while longer? Maybe I can talk just a little bit of sense into that man's head. Lord, I know he'll listen this time if you'll just let me talk to him one more time. (The sisters are lifting her from the alter.) Lord, no! Please not my house! Not my family. Not my husband. Lord! Lord! Lord! (Collapses in the sister's arms. Sisters join in Mother Elque's singing. Singing is louder now and Beth is sobbing as they embrace and attempt to calm her.)

CURTAINS

ACT III
SCENE I

(Act III Scene I takes place back in the LR/DR area of the Anderson's home. It is approximately one month later. The family returns from church to a sparkling clean house and a dinner table set for four. They are shocked as a jovial and cordial Saul emerges from the bedroom off stage.)

SAUL:

Hey! There they are! My lovely family! (Goes directly and hugs and kisses each one on the cheek. They appear unsure of what's going on.) Sit down. Sit down. Rest y'all's tired feet. Here Beth. (Offers a chair) Sit down. Say, ain't that them shoes that's always giving your bunions HELL—oops—I mean a fit. (Beth continues to look baffled) Here, let me help you out of these things. (Pulls off both shoes and begins rubbing her feet.) How that feels, Beth? That feels better, Beth?

BETH:

Saul, what's the matter with you? You show you alright? I don't aim to be mean by you, Saul, but the truth is I can't think of the last time I seen you act like this. Well I can but, too, truth be told, that's how come we got Martha and Josh.

261

SAUL:

(Laughs at Beth's comment.) That's how come we got Martha and Josh. (More laughter followed by a cough then another.) Lord, Beth, you show ain't changed a whole lot in all these years we been together. You always did know exactly what to say to bring a grin to my face. (The kids are in disbelief and are looking very carefully at their father's new behavior).

BETH:

(More sternly) Saul, I done already asked you one time, but you ain't answered me. I asked you is you alright?

SAUL:

Sho' I'm alright, Beth. Why you keep asking that?

BETH:

'Cause I wants to know why you acting like this here, Saul.

SAUL:

(Ignored the question and quickly changed the subject. Walking briskly to the table and coughing as he goes.) And I cooked y'all a good old fashion Sunday home cooked meal too.

MARTHA:

Daddy, I ain't never known you to cook NOTHING—Sunday, Saturday or otherwise!! Something serious must be 'bout to jump off up in here!

SAUL:

Oh, sho', baby girl! Yo' papa can cook up a storm. You'll see. (Saul is obviously nervous and not at ease about something. The family can detect it in his visibly fidgety behavior.) Y'all ain't got to worry about going out to one of them all you can eat buffets today. Daddy done already took care of that. I done cooked up all y'all's favorites for today. I made bar-b-que ribs for your mama, potato salad with extra pickles and pimentos for you, baby girl, black eyed peas for Josh, and, of course, some corn on the cob and thin fried corn bread for me. Oh yeah, I threw in a little extra too. I kinda out did myself. (Martha raises her eye brows as if to ask OH YEAH?) I made a chocolate cake for dessert and old fashion lemonade to (cough) wash everything down with. Now how that sound to y'all? (Waits for a response. Everyone looks one to the other still stunned.) It's all in the stove, so y'all just let me know when y'all's ready to eat and I'll get everything set up in just a short minute. (Cough. Still visibly nervous) But I know y'all all tired after a long day in church, so y'all just go ahead and rest right now. Yeah. Yeah. Y'all rest a spell. Just don't rest so long that y'all lets all that good cooking get all cold before y'all gets any of it in y'all's bellies now.

JOSHUA:

I'm sorry, Dad, but I just can't rest right now.

SAUL:

Why son? What's the matter?

MARTHA:

(sounding almost as if she's angry) 'Cause this ain't no resting situation!

SAUL:

What you mean by that, Martha?

JOSHUA:

Come on, Daddy, you know exactly what she means. Come on! Tell me, when is the last time you cooked a meal for this family? (pause) WHEN?!? I mean we go to church every Sunday—at least every Sunday you give us permission to go worship the other God—and you ain't never even boiled water for tea before. Now all of a sudden you cooking whole meals?

MARTHA:

You trying to poison us or something?

SAUL:

Poison y'all? (compassionately) Martha, how could you even think that? Boy, I tell you what. That girl and her mind. Don't even know how she could'da even thought to say something like that.

MARTHA:

How could I think to say something like that, Daddy? (Approaching Saul slowly and deliberately) How? (Pointing to the scar he left on her face) Look. You see that? And that? (another scar. And look (another scar) And another one too. (Goes over and jerks Joshua by the arm. Pulls him over to his father) And if that's not reason enough look here and here and here and . . .

BETH:

MARTHA!! That's enough of that now.

MARTHA:

No mama I'm not sure it is. You see . . .

BETH:

MARTHA!! I done told you that's enough of that foolishness. Now don't you let me have to say that same thing no mo' girl. I'm sure yo' daddy sees what he done done over all these years. And I'm sho' he be real sorry about it too. But I ain't gonna stand her and just let you tongue lash him to death about it now. You just forgive him now and let bygones be bygones.

MARTHA:

Mama?

BETH:

Yeah, Baby?

MARTHA:

If Daddy is so sorry why you have to do all the apologizing for him? I told ya'll I think the man's up to no good as usual and I ain't 'bout to be part of it neither.

JOSHUA:

So what is it, Dad?

SAUL:

What is what, Joshua?

JOSHUA:

Like Martha said, what are you up to?

BETH:

Children. Why y'all just keep being so hard on your po' Daddy. Can't y'all just accept the fact he done a good deed for us today and he ain't got to be up to nothing?

CHILDREN:

NO!!

BETH:

And why can't ya? (sounding irritated)

JOSHUA:

'Cause we have come to know this man by his deeds, Mama . . . and not by your HOPES and wishes for him. Sure we have all hope for a father who would act this way all our lives, but his DEEDS . . . his abuse, his lying, his deceit, his whoredom, his apathy, his . . .

BETH:

Shut up Joshua! Shut up! I done heard enough of this foolishness for one day. Now I want you and Martha both to just cut out all of this foolish. Just stop it! Y'all complain when you ain't got nobody acting like a daddy and now y'all complaining when you GOT somebody acting like a daddy! There just ain't no satisfying some folks!

MARTHA:

What DADDY Mama! All the man did was cook dinner for the first time in nearly 20 year for God's sake!

BETH:

And don't you start using the Lord's name in vain either young lady! 'Cause I absolutely ain't gonna stand for that in this house! (Tempers are beginning to escalate slowly but steadily.)

JOSHUA:

(Controlled but firm) Oh come on, Mama, don't change the subject. You know what she means.

BETH:

I don't know what she mean NOTHING and I ain't sure I want to neither!

MARTHA:

And that's your problem, Mama! You don't ever want to know anything. But there are things that you do know, Mama and you KNOW you know them. But oh no, you think if you don't say anything about a problem it'll just up and go away all by itself. You think if you pray . . . but don't ACT after you pray . . . some little magical angel will just come down from heaven and land on your shoulder and make everything as sweet as candy land. You think if you just walk around here with HOPE all day every day things will eventually just turn around from bad to good all by themselves! WELL MOTHER THEY WON'T. THEY WON'T! THEY WON'T! THEY WON'T! THAT'S JUST NOT THE WAY THINGS . . . AND PROBLEMS . . . . AND PEOPLE IN THE REAL WORLD GET CHANGED MOMMIE DEAR!!!

BETH:

(Goes to Martha and slaps her firmly across the face.) Don't you EVER raise your voice at me again young lady. You understand that? (Turns to walk off. Two steps. Stops. Martha falls in her mother's arms and they both begin to sob.)

SAUL:

(Goes over and places his hand on BETH's shoulder.) She never yelled at you, Beth. It was me she was yelling at all the time and I knew it. It was my years of neglect. My non-stop drinking. My womanizing. My lies. My broken promises. My being out with the fellows when I should have been in with them. My seeing y'all go off to church but never taking y'all there. (cough) She was yelling at all the times I missed her school plays, track meets, Christmas recitals and honor banquets. She was yelling at all the times you set the table for four buy only the three of y'all showed up to eat. She was yelling at all the times I embarrassed her by showing up and throwing up—drunk and bumbling—in public. (Moves to couch area) I understand at who, what and why Martha was yelling, Beth. And for the first time in my life I see how much confusion, sorrow, torment, shame and hurt I have given all of y'all. (Turns to Beth) So don't hit her Beth. I've done that too much already. Don't yell at her. I've overdone that too. It's not her fault, Beth. It's mine.

BETH:

(Letting go of her daughter as she begins to speak) Saul, maybe you're right . . . and I don't mean to blame you for every that's wrong in this house but . . .

SAUL:

It's not blame, Beth. It's facts. It's the truth. (cough) Beth, I'm the man of this house. And with that title comes a whole lot of responsibilities I haven't even come close to living up to. I've been mean, weak, wicked, destructive and generally unproductive. I know I haven't been a father, a husband, a provider, a friend, or a leader. So now I can't blame my children for not letting one Sunday dinner erase all those years of hurt and neglect.

BETH:

I'm glad you know and understand how all of us feel, Saul. So you ought not to have no problem with me taking my children and leaving you.(Kids looked shocked.)

SAUL:

(Moving to L center stage) Naw, Beth, I ain't got no problem with y'all leaving—except one. (cough)

BETH:

And which one is that, Saul?

SAUL:

It ain't necessary for y'all to leave.

BETH:

Necessary? What you talking about, Saul?

SAUL:

Beth . . . Martha . . . Joshua (gesturing to the LR couch) y'all come on in here and sit down. I got some talking I need to get done. Come on. This won't take long, I promise. (they comply) This ain't easy but one than' for sure and that is bad news sho don't get no better with time. (smiles and fidgets nervously) Beth and Martha and Josh (cough) I didn't mean to but I done went and made breaking this family up mighty easy for all of us. Truth is ain't none of us got to do nothing at all but just wait about sixty to ninety mo' days (cough) and the Lord will break it up for us.

BETH:

Saul what on earth are you talking about? Why I ain't never heard you mention nothing bout GOD or the Lord in yo' life 'cept to tell us YOU is God.

MARTHA:

At least we ain't never heard you mention nothing good about the Lord is what she means.

JOSHUA:

Will everybody just stop talking in circles and just let Dad tell us what it is he wants us to know. (Saul appears nervous and tentative. He is on the verge of tears.)

BETH:

Saul is you leaving us?

MARTHA:

For some other homewrecker I bet.

JOSHUA:

How old is she this time, Dad, 16? 17? Or is she really old this time? You know, around 18 or 19 maybe?

BETH:

(Eyes fixed. Voice monotone.) Josh, you and Martha let yo' daddy talk. I get a feeling way down in my bones 'bout what he fixing to say. Go ahead, Saul. Go ahead. It's ok. The Lord's done already showed me you got news to tell us. Go head, you can tell us now.

SAUL:

For a long time I thought I WAS God. I though could ever happen (cough) to me. I though I could act a fool and be a fool as long as I wanted to and nothing would ever come of it. Then a few days ago I went to the doctors to get checked for this nagging cough . . . (pauses) they tested me and found out I've got advanced liver problems, a chest full of heart problems, and (embarrassed to admit it) later stages of a sexually transmitted disease.

ALL:

A WHAT?!?

SAUL:

The doctor told me I've got probably around 90 nor more than 100 days left to live. Said they done seen all these diseases in this stage too many times before in other people to be wrong. Said I have no chance of surviving cause if one disease don't get me in that length of time, the other one will. I know I ain't been much in the past and I know I ain't got a whole lot of future to make a lot out of myself. But if y'all can just believe I love y'all and I'm sorry for what I've done and let me be a good husband and father for the little while I do have left . . . I'll die a happy and fulfilled man. (Saul stands and waits for a response from his children. They are expressionless. Emotionless. Martha gets up and walks away without a word. Joshua follows. Saul appears crushed. Saul and Beth sit on the couch next to one another. They embrace tightly for a long moment. She gingerly touches his face and hair but says nothing. She kisses the back of his hand. Saul and Beth embraces for a long moment. Again she rubs his hands, face, shoulder and hair. Beth bursts into tears and runs off stage L. Saul looks around. Reflects. Burst into tears while burying is face in his hands.)

CURTAINS

ACT III

SCENE II

(Martha enters from off stage. She sits at the family's dinner table and glares over at her father. He peers up at her then drops his head. She gets up and starts over. Then stops and returns to the table and sits. He notices and speaks.)

SAUL:

You can come on over here, baby girl. I ain't got nothing you can catch just by sitting in the same room with me. (She hesitates then moves to the couch. Saul coughs then continues) You know, Martha I started calling you baby girl right after you was born—17 years ago. I came to the hospital right after yo' mama had you. I wouldda been there during the delivery but I was in the Army then and my old C.O.—commanding officer—well he kinda wouldn't let me leave when I was suppose to in order to be back here on time for your birth.

MARTHA:

(Half angry/half sympathetic) That was kinda of mean of him, don't you think?

SAUL:

Yeah. But it comes with the territory. The Army is about fighting wars and taking lives not arranging flight schedules so soldiers can go home and welcome in a new life. Anyway, I remember walking into that hospital room and seeing the prettiest and proudest wife . . . woman . . . mother in the world. She was laying there holding you in her arms, patiently and lovingly stroking your hair with her pointing finger (he does so to her to illustrate). Oh yeah, baby girl, you was born with a head full of hair. (cough, cough) Everybody use to say that was a sign of good luck. All of a sudden your mother looked up and seen me standing in that doorway with my Army uniform on and a dozen of red roses and her whole face just beamed with pride and joy. She didn't even say hello. She just grabbed you up and held you up in both arms and said to me "It's a baby girl." I was so dumbfound that all I could do was stand there and repeat "baby girl, baby girl, baby girl." A nurse standing by came over and took the flowers out of my hands and went over and placed them down on the bed next to yo' mama. Then she took my baby girl out of yo' mama's arms and brought you across that hospital room and carefully handed you to me. I was too excited to even move. I just kept standing there and repeating "baby girl." Sounds like he's already decided on a nickname for this one the nurse turned around and told yo' mama. Yeah, sounds like it to me too yo' mama said back to the nurse. And from then on you've always been my baby girl.

MARTHA:

That's a beautiful story, Dad. I'm just sorry you never shared that with me before now.

SAUL:

Me too, Martha. (cough) Me too. (Gets up and moves about the stage. Temporary silence.) Martha . . . I just want to tell you I'm sorry.

MARTHA:

So am I Dad. (Gets up and moves about the stage as she knows this is going to be a difficult conversation.)

SAUL:

YOU? What in the world do you have to be sorry for?

MARTHA:

Can we talk, Dad?

SAUL:

Talk? Baby girl, ain't that what we doing right now?

MARTHA:

No. Right now we're reminiscing. But for the first time in my life I need to TALK to—no—WITH (passionately) my daddy. So I need to know, can we talk?

SAUL:

(Nods yes. Coughs) Yes, baby girl. We can talk.

MARTHA:

Daddy (Emotions building.) Daddy . . . Why did you do this to us . . . to me . . . to Mama . . . to Joshua . . . and even to yourself? Why?

SAUL:

Now, Baby Girl, you got to know it wasn't like I went around looking forward to no sickness or disease.

MARTHA:

(Emotionally) BUT YOU DID!! (Beth can be seen standing in the entrance door off stage. She has noticed the conversation between father and child and has opted to allow them time together.) What did you expect to find out there in six or seven different beds a months? What did you expect to find at the bottom of the Jack Daniel bottles you polished off every day for the past several years. What did you expect to find rolled up in a marijuana joint or in the tip of a cocaine needle? What? What? What good did you possibly expect to find . . . DADDY?!?

SAUL:

Baby Girl, . . .

MARTHA:

(Turning and point emphatically) NO!!! You said we could talk! So let's talk! Let's not just talk about the cute little stories about how I received a nickname. Let's not just talk about the missions and the philosophies of the Army. But let's also talk about how I must feel to be losing a daddy I never got a chance to know. And guess what. It wasn't because he was away in Korea either. Let's talk about what kind of a daddy you were when you were healthy and able-bodied and when we could have done fun and memorable things together as a family but didn't because you were in no way interested in spending time with us. (Her voice is growing louder and more emotional with each sentence.) Let's talk about how what you've done to us has and will continue to affect us long after you're dead and gone. (Anger beginning to come through in her voice again. Becoming emotional) Let's not just sit here and talk about all the pretty things in life as if the ugly things never happened! For the first time in my life I want to TALK with you, Daddy. So come on. (Emphatically beneath her breath) Let's talk.

SAUL:

But Baby Girl I'm dying. I ain't got long to be here with y'all no more. (Cough) I don't want to just sit around and talk about all the bad stuff . . . .

MARTHA:

(Interrupting her father) But that's all you lived. That's all you did. That's all you were. That's all I know and remember about you. That's ALL the memories of you I have. That's all you'll ever be to me. (Beth turns and exits the doorway). So what else is there for us to talk about if we can't talk about the truth? I'm sorry, but that is the only daddy I know.

SAUL:

Martha can't you just sympathize with yo' own dying daddy and make yo'self see . . .

MARTHA:

See what? A lie? Why? Because if I CHOOSE to see a lie now that you are sick and supposedly dying, *you* will feel better about your own death? So you would ask me to look at you through these eyes of hurt, disgust, shame, sorrow and rejection and still force myself to see a *lie* after all these years. I can't do that, Daddy. No. Your baby girl can't do that. You see, I've seen too much truth—ugly truth—painful truth—unwanted truth—embarassing truth—over the past 17 years of my life to start seeing lies now. (Goes over to her father) Let me tell you what I see. Alright? I see a man who never attended a single PTA meeting. I see a man who doesn't even know how I'm doing in school, what grade I'm in in school or if I'm even *in* school. I see a man who has no idea whether his own "BABY GIRL" is a virgin or a whore. I see a man who doesn't know if his only daughter wants to grow up to be a doctor or a dike. I see the reason for these bruises. I see a man who has never taken me for a walk in the park, or out to a restaurant for a Sunday evening dinner, or to a matinee movie, or on a summer vacation. When I see you I see a father who has not even taking one hour out of his schedule to even drive his own baby girl to the ice cream parlor, a book store or even to the public library. I see a man who has all my life told me through his actions that hanging out with the boys was more intelligent and important than spending any meaningful time with his son, daughter or wife. I see a man who never heard me lead a song in the church choir or read me a Bible verse in his life. That's what I see. And you know what else I see? I see a man who would rather get high and drunk and beat up on me—an innocent 17 year old 5'4" 125 pound female child—rather than to take the time to teach me and guide me and lead me by example. When I look at you I see a stranger. Sure my daddy—but a stranger. (Becoming increasingly emotional again) Sure, the man who created me—but a stranger. Sure, the man who nicknamed me—but still a stranger. Want me to prove it to you? Alright, *DAD*, answer these questions for me. Who is my boyfriend? Do I have a boyfriend? Is he Black? White? Hispanic? Baptist? Catholic? Pentecostal? Is he a pusher? A pimp? Perhaps a preacher? An addict? A dropout? Or an A student? Last year I won three of the school's highest honors. What were they? Who presented them to me? Next week I will be participating in a national contest. Where is it and what kind of contest is it? Four months ago while you were out there hopping from bed to bed, I had a tumor removed. Can you tell me from where, when I had it done and what doctor did it? How was it paid for? Do you know? Do you care? Did you care then? You see—you are my daddy because biologically you created me. But you're *not* my daddy because you have *fathered* me. Now I respect the fact that you're ill. And I can sympathize with your illness, but please don't expect much more from me than that. Because you see, Daddy, you created this monster (pointing to her heart) . . . now deal with it.

SAUL:

I know you'll mad with me, Baby Girl. And I know you got plenty of reasons to be too. I mean, after all I gave you most of them myself. But still I'm *dying* and I want to get . . . you know close to y'all before . . . I . . . I go. I want us to be a family. To be happy. And to love one another—just one time before I go.

MARTHA:

FOR NINTY OR ONE HUNDRED DAYS? Then what, Dad? For God's sake why haven't you thought of this long before somebody told you you had one foot in the grave and the other on two banana peels. What kinds of happiness is that suppose to bring *us*? And are we suppose to just set aside all the years of abuse and neglect you gave us just so you can "GO" away from here happy? What about the rest of us? How happy do you think we're going to be while we're putting on this great big show for you? If you wanted to die happy you should have lived a "happy" life. If you wanted to die loved you should have loved while you lived. No dad. I'm sorry. I can't—I won't—play that game with you.

SAUL:

Baby Girl, don't you love your daddy? I love you.

MARTHA:

(Extremely angry) YOU WHAT???!!? You *LOVE* me?!? (Laughs loudly)

SAUL:

What are you laughing at? What's so funny about that?

MARTHA:

YOU!! I'm laughing at you. You're a joke! You don't love me! You can't.

SAUL:

What you talking about I can't?

MARTHA:

Dad, love is not in what you say, how you feel, whether or not you're sick or well, your opinions, your education or any of that crap. Don't you know . . . (softly) Love is only in what you DO. So if you beat me—you don't love me.

If you forsake me—you don't love me. If you lie to me—you don't love me. If you fail to teach me, to guide me, to inspire me—you don't love me. If you choose women, drugs and alcohol over me—you love THEM, but you don't love ME. And if I am your child and we are still strangers after living in the same house together for 17 years and you have not bothered to even try to train me up in the way that I should go so that when I am old I will not depart from it—you simply don't love me. And I don't know why even *you* can't see that. (SAUL is speechless. He looks down at the floor)

SAUL:

I'm sorry, Martha. Now I understand why you're so mad with me. And all this time I thought I loved you just because you were my child.

MARTHA:

No daddy. Just like you created me and Josh . . . and had fun doing it . . . (passionately) you have to create and sustain love too. (She goes over and kisses him on the cheek.) Not to worry though. Inspite of it all I still love YOU—as I always have, Daddy—and will be with you until the end. No matter what you have or will ever do to me or this family, nothing in the whole wide world can ever stop me from loving my daddy. Nothing. Nothing that he ever says. Nothing that he ever does. No degree or amount of pain he causes us will ever stop me from loving my daddy. Now that's love, Daddy. That's love. (exits L passes Joshua entering on her way out. Joshua is carrying a tablet in his hand. His father has not yet noticed him. He sits at the table and begins to read quietly from the tablet. Looks over at his father and asks . . .)

JOSHUA:

You feel like talking?

SAUL:

(Noticing his son for the first time) I thought I did until I started listening . . . to what your sister had to say that is.

JOSHUA:

And what was that?

SAUL:

Just some things I wish somebody had said to be a long time ago—BEFORE I started dying. (pause) Josh, what kind of daddy would you say I been to you?

JOSHUA:

(Instantly hears the advice of Mother Elque replaying in his mind: "Joshua, no matter what happens in your life always trust God, take a stand and to thine own self be true.) The same kind of father you've been to Martha, Dad. You know that. One thing about your abusive and neglectful ways is that you were not discriminatory in your practice. You were as neglectful and abusive to me as you were with the women in this house. I'm sorry to have to say that at a time like this, Dad, but it true.

SAUL:

Don't ever be sorry to have to tell the truth, son. After all you didn't make it true, I did. I'm the one who needs to be sorry. Joshua. Josh, how can I make up for all the wrong things I've done?

JOSHUA:

Make up? Dad, I'm 19 years old now. I'm a freshman in college now. How can you possibly make up for all the years you've missed already—especially with just three months left to live. Dad, once you've neglected someone that neglect is forever. You can't go back and undo that. How could you? If you undid that you would be neglecting the present. So how do you ever make up?

SAUL:

I guess the key is to never fall behind, huh?

JOSHUA:

That IS the key, Dad. You see I can't take you back eleven or twelve years ago to Patriot Park when I hit my first T-Ball homerun. And I can't take you back to eight grad honors day when I received two distinguished awards and you weren't there to see me receive them. And I can't take you back to my sophomore high school year when I lost my best friend to a drive by shooting and didn't even know how to deal with that situation. We can't make up for those times, Dad. They're over. They're done. I've made it through all of those times without your help, so please don't make me go back and dig up all of those old and painful memories just so YOU can feel better about dying. I'm sorry, Dad. I can't do that. (Moving about the stage). Now I heard some of your conversation with Martha. I guess I kind'a stood in the doorway to my room and eavesdropped a little on youall's chat. I want you to know Martha is not mad with you she's mad about not ever having had you in her life . . . and now she knows—whether she sees it as good or bad—she's about to lose you again—but this time it's forever. And I feel the same way. (Tosses the tablet to his father)

Here! Read this. It's not really about you. It's more about the daddy I wished you were.

(There is a minute of silence as Saul examines the poem to himself.)

SAUL:

This is beautiful. I never knew you wrote poetry—especially like this.

JOSHUA:

I know, Dad. That's because you know so little about me—or Martha—or Mom. You see the boys, the bottle, the needles, the women, the gambling—they have all made you a stranger to this family. It's so sad you now have come to learn us only when facing death. And sure we believe you are sorry, but that doesn't take away one single pain or bad memory from any of our past. (Saul is speechless. He begins to reexamine the poem.) You like it?

SAUL:

Like I said it's beautiful son. I just wish I could have been this kind of Daddy for you.

JOSHUA:

Yeah. I wish you had CHOSEN to be that kind of Daddy for me too. Then maybe I could see you differently and feel differently about what's going on with you now. (Beth and Martha enter unnoticed and are seated in the kitchen. Saul begins reading the poem "MY DADDY" aloud. They sit attentively while Saul is reading.)

SAUL:

MY DADDY

Who is this man looking at me?
Through whose eyes I will ultimately see,
Myself, the world, and even my own son,
And by whose measures I will someday a man become?

Who is this man looking at me?
Whose hand I hold in pursuit of my destiny,
In whose footsteps I trod seeking to chart my own path
Whose judgment will dictate when to cry and when to laugh.

Who is this man looking at me?
By whose beliefs I will someday decree
Whose word to me is as true as god's own grace,
and to reproach his integrity would be an absolute disgrace.

Who is this man looking at me?
Who never tires nor reneges on his loyalty,
Who reads me books about fairy tales, places, and oceans,
Who is too committed to ever betray his love and devotion.

Who is this man looking at me?
Who has know all about me since my infancy,
Who teaches me not only society's principles, morals and truth
But he also teaches me from Genesis, Leviticus, Matthew and Luke.

Who is this man looking at me?
Who teaches me to look inside myself and see
The good, the bad, the weak, and the strong
That which builds mighty men, that which destroys weak homes.

Who is this man looking at me?
Embracing me tightly as he prays on bended knee
forgetting never his spiritual maker and king
Never ashamed to honor Him daily as he prays and sings.

Who is this man looking at me?
Who constantly encourages me to be all I can be,
Preparing and striving always to be his best
Instilling in me the courage to face any test.

Who is this man looking at me?
My inspiration, my guide, and the leader of my family.
He's my joy and my glory and I hold him up for the whole world to see
The man that I love most—my hero—MY VERY OWN DADDY!

Who is this man looking at me?
Through whose eyes I will ultimately see,
Myself, the world and even my own son,
And by whose measures I will someday a man become.

Who is this man looking at me?
Whose hand I hold in pursuit of my destiny,
In whose footsteps I trod seeking to chart my own path.
Whose judgment will dictate when to cry and when to laugh.

Who is this man looking at me?
By whose beliefs I will someday decree,
Whose word to me is as true as God's own grace,
And to reproach his integrity would be an absolute disgrace.

Who is this man looking at me?
Who never tires nor reneges on his loyalty,
Who reads me books about fairy tales, people and oceans
Who is too committed to ever betray his love and devotion.

Who is this man looking at me?
Who has known all about me since my infancy,
Who teaches me not only society's principles, morals and truth
But he also teaches me from Genesis, Leviticus, Matthew and Luke.

Who is this man looking at me?
Who teaches me to look inside myself and see,
The good, the bad, the weak and the strong,
That which builds mighty men, that which destroys weak homes.

Who is this man looking at me?
Embracing me tightly as he prays on bended knee,
Forgetting never his spiritual maker and king
Never ashamed to honor him daily as he prays and sings.

Who is this man looking at me?
Who constantly encourages me to be all I can be,
Preparing and striving always to be his best,
Instilling in me the courage to face any test.

Who is this man looking at me?
My mentor, my leader, my confidant, and personal honoree,
He's my inspiration and my glory and I give him to the world to see
The man I love—my greatest hero—MY VERY OWN DADDY!!

BETH:

Saul, that was truly beautiful.

SAUL:

Yeah, Beth (starring in dismay at his son) I think so too. Joshua, I just want you to know that I love you son.

JOSHUA:

Remember, Dad, love is ONLY in what you do . . . not in what you say.

SAUL:

(Looking at Martha) Yeah, I kind'a remember hearing that somewhere before. Seems like everybody else realized that all along except me.

JOSHUA:

No, Dad. EVERYBODY realized that—including you. You just *chose* not to show us love. That's all. Truth.

SAUL:

Beth, I ain't never told you this before, but I want to tell it to you right now . . . and that is you show done one hell of a job raising these children. How you did it and put up with me too—I don't know. But Lord have mercy you show did a good job. I'm proud of you, Beth.

BETH:

(Moving into LR area) Well, Saul, I guess I needs to come clean and confess to you too then.

SAUL:

Confess what?

BETH:

Well, Saul, I ain't been raising these children all by myself. You see, when it seemed I had done all but lost you legally, I went out and found me another man just like you found yourself another woman.

SAUL:

You done what?? Another man?? In my house?? With my wife?? Over my children?

BETH:

(Very calm and relaxed) Yeah Saul. Another man. In yo' bed. In yo' house. In yo' bathroom. In yo' kitchen. Wid yo' wife . . . Over yo' children . . . And even with yo' children.

SAUL:

(Visibly upset) WITH MY CHILDREN!!! Now Beth you done went just one step too far now. What kind of woman is you anyhow? Here I been talking about how good a job you done with these children and now you come here telling me 'bout some other man who done been all over my house and sounds like all over my family too.

BETH:

He is Saul. But you ought not to care 'cause I swear, he a real good man, Saul.

SAUL:

GOOD MAN!!!

BETH:

(Still very calm despite Saul's rage.) He feeds us. 'Cause Lawd knows sometimes I know I didn't know where the next food was coming from. He protected us. He nurtured us. He guided us. He slept wid us.

SAUL:

(Pointing his finger at his wife) And that's what I got a problem with right there.

BETH:

(Ignoring Saul's remark) He talked wid us. And he made us love you inspite of all your wrongness. Yeah, Saul, I went out and got Jesus and since I started living with Jesus and he started living with me and these childen, I ain't missed having NO OTHER man since he moved in here. Now I don't never sleep by myself no more, not even on them nights when you be sleeping way cross town wid some other woman. My children got a steady daddy. I got a companion. And my soul is happier than you use to make my body feel when we was having sex. One show thing about Jesus, Saul—he ain't no bi-sexual or nothing like that—but he'll marry you too. He'll sleep with you too. He'll touch you too. He'll heal you too. 'Cause he loves you too. Now I'm telling you what I know Saul. God is real! He ain't to be mocked and played with. But if you can believe in your heart and confess with your mouth Jesus can come into yo' life today and make some mighty big changes. He can come in and become YOUR daddy. But you got to let him.

SAUL:

Beth you know I don't know nothing 'bout no Jesus. I ain't never been no churchgoer in my whole life. I don't know nothing bout how to pray and ask the Lord to do nothing for me.

BETH:

You don't have to know, Saul. All you got to do is to call his name.

SAUL:

That's all? You mean just 'cause I call him . . . he'll come.

BETH:

Well you might have to call him more than one time now, Saul, but he'll come. I know he will. He already done promised us that He'll never leave us nor forsake us. (Begging) Try Him, Saul. Try Him. Just try Jesus.

SAUL:

But how will I know when he done heard me?

BETH:

Saul, we're talking about a REAL god now. You'll know. I promise you that.

SAUL:

(Innocently as he begins to go on bending knees) And I'll know?

BETH:

You better believe it, man. Just call his name and talk to him. It ain't got to be nothing fancy, long or hard. (Martha is entering the kitchen area) Just talk to Him the same way you talk to me. It ain't yo' words He's looking at—it's yo' heart.

MARTHA:

(Coming into the LR area) You can do this, Dad. It really isn't hard. Try it. After all what do you have to lose?

SAUL:

(Looking around at his family) Yeah. And look what all I got to gain.

JOSHUA:

(Comes over and pats his father on the back) Don't worry about a thing; we're right here with you, Dad. Go ahead. Talk to God.

SAUL:

(Saul's head bows slowly as he prepares to pray for the first time in a long time.) Lord, Jesus . . . My family sent me down here to talk to you. Lord, I'm shame to say I don't even know what to say . . . I mean it's been so long since I talked to you and all. But if you'll just let me bend your ear for just a little while . . . I promise you I'll be gone and I won't worry you no more soon. Now Lord . . . (Saul continues to pray as his family gives him encouraging pats on his back and BETH, MARTHA and JOSHUA BEGINS SINGING AN OLD HYMN.)

CURTAINS

ACT III

SCENE III

(Scene III takes place the following Sunday morning at the church. The scene opens with the pastor delivering the morning sermon.)

PASTOR:

So when the doctors tell you that recovery is impossible I tell you, you have placed your faith in the wrong physician. When the situations seems too much for you to bear . . . I tell you that's because you have not learned how to lean on Jesus. For the one writer wrote "What a friend we have in Jesus. ALL our sins and griefs to bear. What a privilege it is to carry . . . EVERYTHING to God in prayer. So whatever it is that you are bearing today, why don't you bring it to the alter and give it over to Jesus. Whatever it is that's burdening your soul why don't you come and give it to Jesus. And so this morning I want to tell somebody who is sick in their body that God is a healer. I want to tell somebody who is going through difficult times that God is a provider. I want to tell somebody who may be saying I just don't know how to believe . . . that God is a teacher. But most of all I want to tell somebody who may be depressed and rejected that God is a forgiving God. And surely you will need him before you leave this world. Now church we're going to have alter call. And we're going to leave it up to each heart to decide if you wish to participate in today's alter call. But I want you all to know one thing as you sit there and ponder whether or not you want to include God in your life . . . People life is too short, death is too certain, hell is too hot and eternity is too long for you to sit there and jeopardize your soul.

(The congregation stands and many of them file out to participate in alter call prayer. They are now singing the alter call songs as they proceed to the altar. Beth and the family momentarily remain in place. Beth finally heads to the altar. Once there and standing Joshua joins her. Seconds later Martha joins them. Martha looks back and extends her hand to her father who appears anxious but reserved about coming to the altar. Finally, in a timid fashion he joins the family at the altar. The Reverend begins to pray.) Father we have come before you with bowed heads but uplifted spirits to ask once again that you protect us from the ways of evil, that you remain the light unto our path, and, Lord, I pray that the power and truth of Your divine, righteous and ever lasting word work a miracle in the life of somebody right now. I pray that you convict their hearts. That you touch their souls. That you anoint their minds. That you guide their feet. And that you heal their bodies. Open their eyes to the truth, the power and the glory of your everlasting righteousness. Forgive them of their transgressions. Wipe their slates clean. Right now, Master. Speak to the righteous ears of their hearts and whisper words of forgiveness to their souls. Let them know that you love them STILL and INSPITE of. Let them know that you loved them even when they lived and wallowed in the pity of sin. Let them know that you welcome them into the Kingdom of Glory despite their past as a faithful servant of iniquity. Dry their tears away right now, God. (Saul wipes tears from his eyes.) Give them a reason to smile—right now, God. Show them that only you can make right in the twinkling of an eye that which they have made wrong over a period of years. Touch families today, God. (Josh puts his arm around his mother's and sister's shoulders. Their heads remain bowed.) Touch Fathers today. Touch mothers today. Touch sons and daughters today, God. (Martha, who is standing between her brother and father puts her arm around her father's waist.) Restore families, Lord. Replace discontent and confusion with love, Jesus. Redeem lost spirits right now, Lord. Bind anger and destruction. Show Satan that he has no victory in your camp, Lord. Beat him away, God. Cast him out, Father. Whip him with the stripes of divine destruction. Then replace his divisiveness with love. (Martha puts her hand around Josh's waist. Saul is doing the same thing at the same time. The two touch hands at the center of their son's back. They join hand and remain so until completion of the prayer.) Replace his lies and deceit with truth. Replace his corruption with honesty. Replace his evil with good. Replace his spirit with that of your own. And then, Father, we know that our souls will be in the safest hands possible when our time has come to leave here. For there are no hands safer than your own. Convict someone now, Lord. For my spirit tells me there's someone standing before you crying out to be convicted. Touch someone now, Lord. For my spirit tells me someone is in need of a touch. Assure someone right now, Lord, for my spirit tells me someone among us is in doubt. Save someone right now, Lord, for my spirit tells me that at least one among us longs to live with you in eternity. And if it be your will—heal the sick right now, Lord. For there are those in need of your healing touch right now. And when you have worked the miracles of your choice in the lives of your choice, teach us to accept your divine guidance and decisions even when they are not as we would have them to be. For we know our ways may twist and turn and our hearts may throb and ache, yet in our souls we are glad to know we are the children of a father who makes no mistakes. In Christ Jesus name we pray . . . And together we say . . .

ALL:

Amen. Amen. (The congregation begins returning to their seats. They are still singing Come To Jesus. Saul stands frozen in place with tears streaming down his face. He has not moved from his position at the altar. He wants to move but appears unable to do so. One verse is sung and a second is begun before the pastor raises his hand and brings the singing to a slow and disharmonious diminished halt. Saul continues to cry and occasionally cough.)

PASTOR:

Brother . . . what is it? Tell us what's going on with you. (Pauses) Are you able to talk right now, Brother? (Pauses) Can you tell you what's going on between you and God right now? (Saul cries out loud.) God loves you, Brother. I don't know who you are or who you were before you came in here this morning but if you want God to he'll fix it so you don't have to leave out of here the same person as when you came in here. (Looks up at the parishioners.) Can I get an amen this morning?

CHURCH:

Amen Reverend. Amen.

PASTOR:

Is that what you want this morning, Brother? Is that what you want God to do for you? (Pauses) Why don't you tell us what it is you want God to do for you? Go ahead. And if you feel that you can't talk to us, then talk to God. Tell him. He'll listen, but not if you don't talk to him. Brother, listen to the words of this songs. (MUSIC. While the pastor is singing Saul turns and faces the audience. He covers his face with his hand and sits on the alter Saul before he finally bursts into tears. As soon as the selection is over he embraces the pastor tightly and confesses very tearfully and emotionally . . .)

SAUL:

All I want is my life back. Lord, please just give me my life back. Just let me have one more chance to be a father and a Christian. Just let me have one more chance—just one more year to spend with my family. Give me one more chance to worship you. Lord I'll keep Your commandments. I'll practice Your will. I'll live by Your faith. I'll do as You command me to do. I'll go where You want me to go. I'll do anything You want me to do. I'll say whatever You'll have me to say. Lord, I'll be the very best daddy in the world. I'll be a husband like no other. I'll be warrior on Your Holy battlefield every single minute of my life. Lord, I confess I have sinned against you. I have blasphemed your name. I have committed adultery. I have stolen and I have lied. But now God I'm in need of Your help. I can't make it without You. I can't love my wife without You. I can't be a father to my children without You. I can't correct the errors of my past without You. I need You, Master. You see now I know who God REALLY is . . . and I know it ain't me. I know in whose hands the power truly lies and I know it ain't in mine. I know the Creator and the created and I know which one I am. And, Lord, I know the weak and I know the strong . . . and it is the weak who is now begging the strong for help. Lord, don't leave me. I need You. They need You. We need You. Lord, help me. Forgive me. Heal me. Save me. Keep me. Just don't forsake me. I'll let the alcohol go. I'll let the adultery go. I'll let the gambling go. I'll let the drugs go. But Lord I just don't want to let You go. No more. I've done that much too long and too often already, Lord. I'll been a fool much too long. I've been a sinner much too long. I've been lascivious much too long. I've been perverse much too long. But right now I ask that You give me a rebirth. I ask that you create in me a clean heart. I ask that You renew in me a right spirit. I ask that You blow into me a new breath. I ask that You place in me a new will. (tears and crying) Cause, Lord, I don't want to die the wretched sinner that I am. I'm filthy, Lord. I'm unfit. I'm unsaved. I'm unwashed. My own family . . . well I can understand how they feel and why they feel that way. Lord, I ain't ready to die. I thought I was LIVING. I thought I was GOD. I thought I could just do anything I wanted for as long as I wanted. But in yYour own time and in Your own way You showed me who really is God.

(Light change color. A bright light shines directly on Saul. The remainder of the church is darkened.)

VOICE:

Saul? (Saul looks about baffled) Saul? (Saul continues to look around for the source of the sound) Saul. Now you see I AM for real.

SAUL:

God? Where are you? I mean I hear you but I can't see you.

VOICE:

You have always seen me, Saul, you have just always failed to acknowledge me. I am everywhere and everything that is beautiful and kind, Saul. But I am nowhere nor nothing that is devious or corrupt. You CAN see me, Saul. Look at a father loving his family . . . I am the love you see. Look at a husband loving his wife . . . I am the bond you see. Look at the old teaching the young the spirituality of life . . . I am the knowledge of correctness they receive. Observe the happiness of a little black baby and a little white baby playing together in a sandbox on the playground . . . I am the absence of prejudice you see. Notice those among you sharing their prosperity with the poor . . . I am the compassion you see. See those whom others hate and spitefully use yet they are fair by them in anyway . . . I am the fairness you see. You see Me, Saul. You have always seen me, Saul. For I do not chose to hide myself from you. You have looked upon Me and yet said I do not exist.

SAUL:

But if you saw me in my sin and in my corruption and in all my wrong doings . . .

VOICE:

And I did, Saul.

SAUL:

Why didn't you stop me.

VOICE:

Sin stops sinners, Saul. For I have written and given to you in my word that the wages of sin is death.

SAUL:

You mean you would let me die before you stopped me.

VOICE:

No, Saul. Sin and Satan would let you die before they would allow you to choose me. Again, Saul, in my word I told you clearly to "Choose you THIS DAY whom you will serve." The wages for your services will be paid by your master whom you have served. You, Saul, chose sin as your master and now your wages are death.

SAUL:

But if you're God you can change that.

VOICE:

And as sure as you're Saul you too could have changed that long ago.

SAUL:

But I never knew how.

VOICE:

(Very sternly) Saul!! Never! Never! Lie to God.

SAUL:

Oh, God, please! You've got to help me.

VOICE:

I did help you, Saul. I sent you all kinds of signs.

SAUL:

Signs? What kinds of signs are you talking about?

VOICE:

I touched your body and produced pain to indicate to you that your drinking was hurting you. I gave you a cough to further say to you something is going wrong. I took your appetite to cause your hungry body to turn away from food which is not natural for man to do. I caused your family to love you inspite of your obvious perverse ways. I made you think of your children when you weren't with them so that you would want to be with them more. I gave you a faithful spouse. I sent your children to talk with you though YOUR GOD told you to tell them you didn't have time. I protected you all these years and now you ask me . . . what signs?

SAUL:

Lord, I didn't know.

VOICE:

So you forsook your family because you didn't know?

SAUL:

B-b-but . . .

VOICE:

And you beat your wife—my own beloved child—because you did not know?

SAUL:

L-l-lord . . .

VOICE:

And you lived a life of iniquity, because you did not know?

SAUL:

But I . . . But I . . . But . . .

VOICE:

You violated your body—the temple I gave you— with alcohol and drugs because you did not know? You committed adultery because you did not know? You lied and cheated and stole because you did not know? You committed adultery and blasphemed my holy name because you did not know? You failed to worship me or to even let your family do so at times—because you didn't know? (pause) You have worked the works of YOUR god, Saul, and now he has rewarded you justly. Now depart from me, you worker of iniquity, I know . . . you . . . not.

SAUL:

But Lord you can't do this to me. You can't leave me like this. I know I was wrong but . . . can't you give me just one more chance?

(Stage lights are coming up/spot light is dying down.)

VOICE:

I know you not.

SAUL:

(Pointing to the choir stand) Lord, I'll sing in your choir.

VOICE:

I know you not.

SAUL:

I'll preach your word to all the world!

VOICE:

I know you not.

SAUL:

I'll praise your name.

VOICE:

I know you not, Saul. I know you not. For my word is true and everlasting. My word is the grace by which you must live and not just the comfort with which you must die. Depart from me, Saul. I know you not.

SAUL:

Lord, please don't leave me like this. Here. Here. I'll go down on my knees and call your name and ask You for forgiveness. (Kneels at the altar) See. Lord,

I'm trying. Lord please forgive me! (crying) Forgive me. Lord please don't forsake Your child now. Please! Ple-e-e-ase! (Pastor goes over and puts his arm around Saul, helps him up and begins to talk with him.)

PASTOR:

Brother, are you alright?

SAUL:

No sir, Pastor.

PASTOR:

Why not? What's the matter?

SAUL:

(Tearfully) He told me to depart from him 'cause I'd been a worker of iniquity.

PASTOR:

He WHO, Brother?

SAUL:

(Looking half confused that the pastor doesn't already know.) God!! Didn't you hear him? Did you just hear me talking to God just a minute ago? Didn't you?

PASTOR:

Brother, I believe *you're* talking to God alright, but I believe it's your conscience that's talking back to you.

SAUL:

My conscious?

PASTOR:

You see, brother, God would never tell you to depart from him while you are still alive. He seeks to draw all men closer unto him. God teaches us to repent of our sins and transgression and that he will forgive us—several times each day. My brother, God is so married to the backslider that his word teaches us that all of heaven rejoices when just one sinner gets saved.

SAUL:

Then you mean all is not lost yet? You mean I could still repent and be forgiven?

PASTOR:

Let me say it this way. No one is hopelessly lost. God is married to the sinner—and so much so that He has written that all heaven rejoices when just one backslider returns to Him. (Taking him by the arm and leading him to the altar for prayer.) I think the Master wants you to get your soul right and right now. And I also think you know this is what He wants from you too. Right?

SAUL:

Right.

PASTOR:

But if you think *your* way who wins, God or Satan?

303

SAUL:

Satan.

PASTOR:

And who loses?

SAUL:

God.

PASTOR:

And . . . ? (pointing to Saul)

SAUL:

Me.

PASTOR:

So who do you think told you to depart from God because you were such a bad person?

SAUL:

(Enlightened) Satan. But how? I was praying to GOD not Satan. How could he do that?

PASTOR:

Brother we battle not against flesh and blood but against principalities of the spirit world. Just know that God will never forsake you. He'll never leave you alone. He'll forgive you of all your sins. He'll wash you, keep you, protect you and guide you every step of the way. Let no man or demon entice you to depart from God. There is none so wrapped up, tied up and tangled up in sin and corruption that God can't clean them up. (Starts escorting Saul back to his seat.) You just continue to pray and remain faithful to the word of God and he will remain faithful to you as well. (Saul gets back to his seat and gives Martha a hug. Pastor returns to the pulpit.) Let us remember our special youth and family services tonight. I am sure God will be present and will work a much needed miracle in somebody's life. We ask that youall please come back tonight and be sure to bring the whole family with you. (To Saul) You too brother.

SAUL:

Oh yes sir, pastor. They'll be here tonight. I promise. (To Beth) No matter what I want my family in church tonight. No matter what.

PASTOR:

May we stand (Audience stands and begins singing one verse of Bless Be The Tide That Binds. They finish.) May the words of my mouth

AUDIENCE:

May the words of my mouth

PASTOR:

And the meditation of my heart

AUDIENCE:

And the meditation of my heart

PASTOR:

Be acceptable in thy sight, O Lord

AUDIENCE:

Be acceptable in thy sight, O Lord

PASTOR:

My redeemer and my strength, Amen

AUDIENCE:

My redeemer and my strength, Amen

(Parishioners turn and hug one another. Casual chatter breaks out and does light laughter between whisper-tone interchanges.)

CURTAINS

ACT III

SCENE IV

(Scene four takes place back in the family home. They have just returned from church and are entering their home in a upbeat and festive mood.)

BETH:

Whew!! Lawd what a day what a day. And didn't the pastor preach a sermon today? Lawd, I tell you, it's been some time since I heard that old rascal wale like that.

(The children enter and go immediately off stage into their rooms. Saul sits at the dining room table. Martha slips out of her shoes and begins to pour two glasses of tea)

MARTHA:

(From off stage) You right, Mama. It's been nothing but time since I heard that man preach and pray like (entering onstage having changed from her church dress and shoes) he did this morning.

JOSH:

(Entering on stage minus his neck tie. Wearing house shoes also.) Yeah!! But it sure sounded good to me. Kind'da need a sermon like that every now and then just to keep you on your toes—against the devil that is.

SAUL:

(Between sips of tea) Either that or on your knees with the Lord. (laughs)

BETH:

Lawd, it's such a beautiful day I thought we might all go and pile up in that old ragged car and go for long cozy family-type ride through the country.

MARTHA:

Family type ride? What kind of ride is that?

JOSH:

Must be the kind of ride they use to go on when Ma and Dad were small. Family type ride. (laughter)

BETH:

Now you hush up yo' mouth now Josh 'cause you know exactly what I mean.

SAUL:

Well, baby, I know what you mean, too, but I ain't really interested in going on no family type ride today.

BETH:

You ain't? I just thought that since the weather was so nice and all.

SAUL:

Well I know what you thought and all. But I got myself another thought.

BETH:

Oh you do now, do you?

SAUL:

Sure do. How about us all going for a family-type walk. Then I'll get the chance to strut down the street with my beautiful wife and my handsome and my baby girl and let folks see just how lucky—uh—blessed I am to have such a beautiful and wonderful family. I think it's been plenty long enough since this community seen this family altogether and acting like a real family. (Get's up and walks over to the living room couch) You see, I'm the man in this house. And if some changes—right changes that is—are going to be made in this house then they gotta start with me. And the first change I want to make is to always make time to spend with my family.

BETH:

Oh Saul . . .

MARTHA:

Daddy . . . That was the sweetest thing I've heard you say since you told me the story about how I got my nickname.

SAUL:

I love you, baby girl.

MARTHA:

(Deep breath) Well . . . judging by what you DO now, and not so much what you say, I'm now beginning to believe it. You know, It's great to have a daddy for once. (Goes over and gives her dad a hug.)

SAUL:

Well don't get use to the daddy you got now. 'Cause the daddy you got now is just a rookie at this thing. You just wait until I done got some more experience at it. Baby girl, me and you gonna go Christmas shopping every year together. And me and Josh gonna go stomping through the woods looking like Paul Bunyan looking for just the right Christmas tree to cut down and bring home. And me and your mama gonna take a week's vacation somewhere every year from now on out. And this is the last Sunday I want you to slave over a stove in this house, Martha. Sunday is the Lord's day. It's the Sabbath. (Josh goes over and is looking out the door. He is looking skyward.) The Lord told us to rest and keep His day Holy. And that's exactly what we're going to do. From now on we eat out EVERY Sunday after church. And Josh Spot needs hisself a new dog house too. Me and you better get that done some time this week.

BETH:

Now Saul don't go and overload yourself. You got plenty of time to take care of all thangs.

SAUL:

I know. I know. But I kind'a get excited when I start acting like a real daddy. It . . . you know . . . make me feel good. You know make me feel like . . .

MARTHA:

A father?

SAUL:

Yeah. That's it. A father. But Beth you ain't heard nothing yet . . .

MARTHA:

(HEADS OVER TO THE WINDOW TO OBSERVE THE WEATHER.)
Well, I just heard something. And I see something too. I heard thunder and I
see dark storm clouds gathering. And they sure don't look good either. I hates
them bad storms. Seems like something bad other than just the weather always
comes alone with them.

JOSH:

Well you're right in this case, Mama. That storm just caused us our first family
walk. I guess we'll just have to walk around and be proud of ourselves next
week, huh? Wh-o-ooa!! And here comes the rain just pouring down like kittens
and puppies.

MARTHA:

That's cats and dogs, Josh.

JOSH:

(Tremendous thunder sound) And there goes the thunder. And
AAr-r-r-r-r!!(Josh is thrown back across the room).

BETH:

(Races across the room to Josh who is lying on his back half dazed) Josh! Josh!
Answer me. Josh!

SAUL:

Josh, are you alright?

JOSH:

(Head resting on his mother's knee. Eyes are stretched big) Did you see that?

MARTHA:

What happened?

JOSH:

That bolt of lightning. It was coming straight for me and I didn't have time to move. Then all of a sudden it reached me and (draws a right angle with his hand) just angled and went directly into the ground right in front of the door. Ain't never seen nothing so weird in all my life.

BETH:

(Looking very bewildered) Storm clouds. Thunder. Lightning striking right on our door steps. Oh Lord. Lord. Please. Not now Lord. (Get up and walks away. Sits at the dinner and rests her head on the table.)

MARTHA:

What's the matter with you, Mama?

BETH:

Nothing baby. Let's just be faithful to God in all things and pray for strength to weather the storms of life. Just be faithful and call on Him in your times of trouble and He will deliver you.

JOSH:

What you talking about, Mama? We ain't got no trouble. This the happiest this family been in our whole life.

SAUL:

We all have strength, Beth. This family's storm done already been withstood. What is there to worry about anyway, Beth? It's just a summer thunderstorm. We done seen a thousand of'em if we done seen one. Ain't nothing for nobody to get all worked up over. It'll be all over after while. (Quickly changes the sullen mood) Now, Josh, you look like you'll alright. Is that right?

JOSH:

(Standing up and brushing off the seat of his pant) Sure! You don't think a few thousand volts of electricity can hurt me do you?

SAUL:

Well since we ain't going walking how about me beating you real quick in a game?

JOSH:

(Holding up cards, checkers, and other games.)

All I can say is choose the battlefield on which you wish to die!

MARTHA:

Make it checkers and I'll play the winner.

SAUL:

Winners it is for my baby girl. (Beth is still sitting along at the end of the kitchen table staring wide-eyed at the family and Saul in particular.) Hey, baby, how about a slice of that good coconut cake you baked last night? You reckon the two men folks in the house can get one of ladies to get that for us since we in the middle of a real important game over here? (Laughter)

BETH:

Cake? Sure Saul. Is there anything else I can do to help make you comfortable? (She appears very dazed. The remainder of the family is now around the checkers board in the living room. Martha goes over and turns on the radio. There is a thumping tune playing. Martha starts to dance.)

SAUL:

Now, Josh, you just gonna have to excuse me a minute 'cause I just can't stand to see my little baby girl dancing all by herself. (Whispering to Josh) Besides that I already promised her I wouldn't ever let her dance by herself again as long as I'm here.

JOSH:

It's all good, Dad. Now I get to eat both pieces of cake while y'all dancing. Oh God. Is that what you call dancing? Oh yeah, I forgot to tell you, Martha.

MARTHA:

Tell me what?

JOSH:

Dad ain't danced since they celebrated.

MARTHA:

They who, Josh? And celebrated what?

JOSH:

Since they the Hebrew children crossed over the Red Sea and celebrated their escape from Egypt! (Laughter) Oh! Oh! Look at him! He's trying some new moves! Don't even try it, Dad. You're only going to end up throwing your back out or straining a muscle or something.

SAUL:

Try it? Son I have you know I'm the one who taught James Brown how to slide, Tom Jones how to glide and Elvis how to titillate from side to side. (He performs a quick dance move which looks like a combination of all three. He's now out of breath.) Baby girl, either my breath is too short or that record is just TOO long. But your old man is gonna have to leave that dance half done for now. But don't worry, I promise to make up the rest of it before we head out to church tonight. Whew-w-w. Man! I must be getting old! (Sits and accepts tea and cake from his wife)

BETH:

That's a terrible storm you know.

SAUL:

Sure is. I usually hate them, but for some reason I feel awfully at peace with this one. An unusual kind of peace. (Lightening is heard striking nearby.)

BETH:

That's good, Saul. It makes me happy that you do. I'm glad to know you've finally found real peace.

MARTHA:

Whose move is it anyway? I thought that game would be over by now. (A tremendous lightening strike is heard. Beth looks up quickly. Saul's eyes catch Beth's. Beth is not surprised. She has been expecting this since the arrival of the storm. Saul's mouth moves as if he's trying to speak but cannot. He lifts his head slightly, flashes a half smile and dies gazing into Beth's eyes. Another tremendous lightening strike is heard. Beth shudders, but says nothing. She continues to stare into her deceased husband's eyes.)

MARTHA:

Is anyone *ever* going to move again in that checkers game?

JOSH:

Hey, it ain't my move. It's the pro's move. The man who taught James Brown how to slide, Tom Jones to glide and Elvis how to move from side to side. Say Dad, what's up with the delay? Come on (lifting his eyes from the checkers board to see his father's distant stare. Martha is still dancing alone. She is yet to notice her father.) . . . Daddy? (Noticing his father and sensing something is wrong. Becoming emotional and nervous.) Daddy!! Mom what's wrong with him?!! DAD!! (shaking him. Martha notices and turns off the music. She hurries half way across the floor. Abruptly stops then proceeds slowly and meticulously the remainder of the way. Meantime Josh is still emotional. Josh is still yet to observe his mother. He has been fixed on his father all this time.) Mom I asked you a question! What's the matter with (noticing Mom's stare for the first time. His voice breaks and calms) . . . Dad. Mama? (See strange look on her face. Gets up and starts across the floor to her.) Mama? What is it Mama?

BETH:

(Martha is frozen and unsure just what to say or how to take this situation. Beth is still frozen and starring into the eyes of Saul. Her voice is prophetic and soft.) The first lightning strike you heard was God's warning that the death angel was headed this way. The second lightning strike meant the death angel was here. The third one meant the death angle had done its job and was on its way back home—the other side of the Jordan—with a soul in tow. Not too long from now you'll hear one more big clasp of lightning. That'll mean the death angel and yo' daddy's soul done both made it cross the Jordan River.

MARTHA:

Then what, Mama?

BETH:

That's when his soul's gotta come befoe' the true and ever living God and face judgment—like all of us got to do sooner or later. I just pray he be alright. That's all. Just alright. (She finally breaks her stare and goes over and touches his hand and closes his eyes. The kids are dumbfounded.) Just call on God in yo' times of trouble and he will deliver you.

MARTHA:

Wh . . . Wh . . . What . . . What right did he have to do that?

BETH:

Do what, baby girl?

MARTHA:

Just come (motioning) waltzing in here (growing emotional and crying) . . . in our home . . . and to just take my daddy away like that! What right did he have to do it, Mama?

BETH:

Baby girl, God's got all rights to do anything in the creations He wants to. He's God. Who is He gonna ask for permission? Beside, honey, death is as much a part of living is living itself (Calm and unemotional).

MARTHA:

THAT'S MY POINT, MAMA!!! WE NEVER LIVED!! WE NEVER GOT A CHANCE TO LIVE!! AND NOW JUST WHEN WE *GET* READY TO LIVE (GESTURING AGAIN) IN WALKS DEATH RIGHT OFF THE STREETS OF . . . OF . . . OF . . . WHEREVER HE'S FROM AND JUST SNATCHES MY DADDY RIGHT OUT OF OUR LIVES. (holding her hands out. She is very distraught).

BETH:

Baby girl, death is only a soldier who takes orders from a higher officer.

MARTHA:

(Extremely emotional) Well I'm going to be a higher officer now. I'm going to give some orders in here. (Goes over and crouches at the feet of her father who remains in an upright seated position.) Daddy . . . Get up. Please. Daddy . . . Open your eyes, Daddy. No Daddy you . . . you . . . you can't go now. You can't leave us. You can't leave me. Come on this is me—Baby girl. Daddy come on (runs over and turn the music back on and begins dancing). I'm . . . I'm . . . I'm dancing by myself again Daddy. Remember you said you would never let your little girl dance by herself again. You said we would finish our dance today, Daddy. You said it! You said it! You promised me! (Josh has crossed the room. Turns off the music. He grabs her about the shoulders . . .)

JOSH:

Martha . . .

MARTHA:

(Ignoring Josh and pushing him away. Crosses to the front door.) Daddy! The rain stopped. We can go for that family walk now. Just like you promised.

BETH:

He can't walk no more, Baby Girl.

MARTHA:

Then we'll go for that long Sunday evening family drive you just told us about. (Suddenly a loud clasp of lightning is heard. Beth immediately lifts her eyes then refocuses on Martha. Very calmly she tells her . . .)

BETH:

He won't be driving no more either, Baby Girl.

MARTHA:

Just don't go, Daddy. Please. Don't go. I'll forgive you of everything if you please just don't go. I'll forgive you, Daddy. I promise I will . . . if you'll just stay a little while longer.

JOSH:

He can't stay, Martha; he's already gone. Our dad is gone.

MARTHA:

(Looking up) Daddy, if you love me come back and stay with us just a little while longer. I've still got a lot to talk to you about. We never caught up on (laughs) the good old times. I never told you about the time I burned my stomach on the stove, or the time I ran off the road and into a ditch trying to miss a stupid old jackrabbit. And I didn't tell you about Josh and his girl friend. And I didn't tell you about the first time I ever kissed a boy (voice and hope and noticeably fading.) And I never told you about the times I cried and cried and cried because I wanted my daddy here with me. I never told you, Daddy. I never told you. I never told you! (She finally touches his cheek and accepts the inevitable). And now after all those years of waiting, painful memories, and tears of hurt and

shame, I guess I won't ever get a chance to tell you, huh? (Gets up and walks around the stage. Family members are quiet.) Isn't that ironic? This man was perfectly healthy and lived for many years and could have been an excellent father, but chose to be and do otherwise. And now just when he decides to put away his childish ways, his foolish ways, his destructive ways . . . and become a father . . . guess what happens? . . . he leaves us again. And this time for good. Well you know something? Know something? I'm DAMN GLAD he's gone. I'm glad he won't be here to hit us and . . . leave us . . . . and come back to us . . . and leave us again . . . and come back again . . . . and leave us again!! (Beth attempts to console her but she pushes away and crosses over behind the couch and talks over her father's shoulder to him) I'M GLAD IT'S OVER! I'M GLAD I KNOW HE'S GONE FOR GOOD AND WON'T BE BACK EVER AGAIN. I'M GLAD I KNOW I HAVE NO DADDY NOW SO I HAVE NO MORE REASON TO HOPE AND WAIT AND PRAY AND WATCH THE DOOR HOPING HE'LL COME HOME JUST ONE MORE TIME! I'M GLAD!!! (To her father) So go ahead and leave us, *DADDY*. Isn't that what you've always done? Isn't that the kind of daddy you've always been? Isn't that when you were always happiest . . . when you were away from us. What did I ever do to you to deserve this? Why didn't you love me before now? Why didn't you spend time with me before now? Why didn't you say I Love You, Baby girl before now? Why didn't we sit and talk before now? Why didn't I have a daddy—BEFORE NOW? (Sits on the couch with her head bowed.)

JOSH:

Martha you got to try and understand . . .

MARTHA:

NO-o-o-o-o!!!!! No!! (Holding her head) I don't understand any of this! Live like an undesirable reprobate and nothing happens to you. Become a decent person—a father—and die instantly. A week and a half ago some know-it-all doctor told that man (pointing to her father) that he had ninety days to live. Now eleven days later all that's remaining is his body and abandoned dreams. (Stands up middle stage and begins dialoguing with God. Joshua goes over and makes a phone call to the ambulatory services.) God, how could you? How could you? JUST when he (Pointing to her father) starting acting like a daddy. *JUST* when he started to love us. *JUST* when the family was beginning to get over some of the hurt and shame and disappointment of so many years of torture and abuse. *JUST when I* was about to have a real daddy for the first time in my life . . . you come in and take him away. And now all I'm left with are the memories of what could have been. The walks we could have taken. The drives we could have driven. The smiles we could have shared. The father-daughter secrets we could have kept. The laughter we could have experienced. God . . . why? Why? WHY? (A spotlight suddenly comes up on Martha. Stage goes dark. A voice is heard.)

VOICE:

Martha, the ways and thoughts of man are not my ways and thoughts. I am alpha and omega, Martha. I was here before all else. I created space and decorated it with the firmaments. I lit the universe with the sun. I hollowed out seas with a gentle press of my finger. Mountains bulged alongside my feet as I walked. I blew breath into clay and called it man. I tell the clouds when to water the earth. I command the winds to blow and tell from whence to come. I cause the seas to rise then instruct them to peace be still. I give life and number days, Martha. Be still and know that *I AM GOD!*

MARTHA:

But, Lord, I thought you loved us.

VOICE:

My love is not as you know love to be Martha. Your love has been taught by the mouths of unrighteous tongues. But my love is the love that permitted me to give my only begotten son for the sins of many who are yet unborn. My love is the love that caused my son while dying on Calvary Hill to beg forgiveness for his killers. My love is the love that caused dry bones to get up and walk, deaf ears to open and receive sound, dumb mouths to speak, barren bodies to give birth and souls to be saved. My love, Martha, is pure and unconditional. It is powerful and perfect. It is tenacious yet tender. My love . . . my ways . . . my thoughts . . . are all beyond the understanding of even the most upright and learned man. Therefore I understand your hurt, my child, but I encourage you, if you love me then trust that I am God and can do no wrong.

MARTHA:

But why my daddy, God, and why now?

VOICE:

Trust that I am God and can do no wrong.

MARTHA:

But couldn't you at least have taken him just a little bit later, God?

VOICE:

Trust in the truth that I am God and can do no wrong.

MARTHA:

I trust you God . . . but will he be okay? I mean his judgment and all.

VOICE:

The great and the small shall be judged and rewarded for their deeds.

MARTHA:

But he repented.

VOICE:

Trust that I am God and can do no wrong.

MARTHA:

I trust you, God. I do. (lights return to the stage. A knock is heard at the door. Josh goes over and opens the door. Ambulance attendance enter and begin to remove the body on a stretcher. Martha runs over and stops them. She removes the sheet from his face. She touches his face lightly and begins to speak.) Daddy . . . (Suddenly a big clasp of thunder is heard. Everyone on stage except Beth jumps as if startled. Beth does not move. She appears to have been expecting to hear the thunder. Martha and Joshua instantly look to their mother for an interpretation.)

BETH:

(Nervously but extremely composed) They made it across the Jordan . . . (A moment of silence ensues as no one knows just what to say. Suddenly another loud clasp is heard. The children look to Beth again.) and now judgment has begun.

JOSHUA:

Will he be okay, Mama? I mean . . . .

BETH:

I know what you mean, son. But that's something I have no way of knowing. There are some things the Lord don't reveal to nobody except himself. It's all in the His hands now. At this point, it's too late to start something new, let go of something old, or do what you should have done years ago. Once you get to the other side of Jordan your judgment is about what you've *already* done, and not about what you had planned to do. Let not your heart be troubled, children. Y'all just be still and know that God is God. Pray for yo' daddy's soul and trust that God will be true to his word to the very end. Go ahead now. (Nods towards Saul's body inviting them to say good bye. Both kids go over and hug the body.) Make peace with his body and let these men be on their way.

JOSHUA:

Why do you say make peace with his *body*, Mama? Why don't you say make peace with *him*?

BETH:

'Cause you can't, baby. You can't make peace with nobody that's already on the other side of Jordan. Peace got to be made here and taken over there with you when you go. (The kids go over and hug the body. Joshua pulls the sheet back over his father's face and nods to the attendant. They leave quietly and close the door. Joshua goes over to the table behind the couch and picks up the pistol his father brandished earlier. He says nothing but waves it back and forth in the same manner and his father at the end of Act I Scene II. His sister notices him.)

MARTHA:

J-J-Joshua. What are you doing? Joshua?

BETH:

(Very concerned) Son, what's the matter?

JOSHUA:

(Still brandishing the pistol but speaking very calmly.) He said he was god.

BETH:

(Tearfully) I know, son.

JOSHUA:

He said he would life forever . . .

BETH:

I know Joshua.

JOSHUA:

And ever . . .

BETH:

Yes he did, son.

JOSHUA:

FOREVER MAMA!!! FOREVER!!! Isn't that what he said? Isn't that what he said just days ago?

BETH:

(Starts over to console her son) Joshua listen to me baby . . .

JOSHUA:

No!! NO!!! NO!!! NO Mama!! (calms down but still emotional) I can't listen. If I listen it hurts more. I remember more. I want more.

MARTHA:

I know what you mean, Josh, but we've just got to go on. We can do it.

JOSHUA:

But couldn't I just have just a little while longer with him? I mean couldn't I just get to know him just a little bit better? Couldn't I get to spend just one more week with him? Couldn't I play just one more game of chess with him? Couldn't I? Why not? Couldn't I? Please. Please?

BETH:

Our days are assigned and numbered, son. God grants any two people just so many days together here on this earth. It's how you spend them together is what makes all the difference in the world. Don't fret. Don't doubt and don't question God. His ways are not like ours, but they are always right.

JOSHUA:

Darn it, Mama!! Can't you stop philosophizing and just answer me. For goodness sake! My daddy just died and I need your help. I need somebody to talk to. I need somebody to lean on. I need somebody to understand.

MARTHA:

I'm here, Josh. You can always talk to me.

BETH:

And the Lord. You see when that man wasn't here I felt the same way you feeling right now. Many a nights I cried and I cried . . . until I found the Lord. And since that time my life been just fine. Now I love your daddy like no other; and never have there been a more dedicated and truer woman to her man than I was to him. But when I needed him, he was never here, and so I had to learn how to turn whole heartedly to another man called Jesus. And by his love and grace and strength, I been kept through it all. So when you look to me for strength and compassion and companionship, I ain't got no choice but to direct you to the same one who had to be all those things for me, when I was too weak to be any of them for myself. Be strong and of good courage, and no matter the situation, children, count it all joy in the Lord.

MARTHA:

Mama, are you telling us that we shouldn't grieve for daddy?

BETH:

No I ain't.

JOSHUA:

Are you saying that we shouldn't be hurt and sad?

BETH:

No I ain't. In the natural you gonna be that way. That was your daddy.

MARTHA:

Then what are you telling us, Mama? What are you telling us we should be feeling right now?

BETH:

Yo' feelings is yo's. You can't help how you feel sometimes. I'm telling you God worked a miracle in this family before he took Saul away from here. I know he did. So I'm just gonna be pleased with the miracle and leave divine business to the divine one. And I advise y'all to do the same thing. (Sounding sanctimonious) It's alright to cry sometimes. We all do. Even Jesus wept. When he seen Lazarus laying there dead his body wept. But then he dried them tears away and said now let me be about my spiritual business. And that's when he called Lazarus! Lazarus! Oh Lazarus! Come forth! And the dead man rose to life. Now somewhere and somehow God called yo daddy . . . Saul! Saul! Oh Saul!! Come forth! And the man inside of Saul rose and went to answer the Lord's call. He had to—cause when the Lord calls, we all have to answer—and go see what he wants. And that's what yo' daddy just did. He didn't do nothing but go to answer the Lord's call. So y'all wipe yo' tears. I believe everything over there is gonna be alright, just fine. I believe God is better at judging when the grapes of his vineyard are ready to be plucked than me and you.

MARTHA:

So he's okay, Ma?

BETH:

We pray he is, Baby girl. We pray he is. Listen here. Why don't you two go to your rooms and just relax for awhile. And don't y'all forget yo' daddy said he wanted us in church tonight no matter what; and that's exactly where we gonna be too. If that's where he wanted his family to be tonight then that's where his family's gonna be. Y'all be careful not to wrinkle up yo' church clothes. Go 'head now. Go head. (They start off L. Martha stops and asks her mother . . .)

MARTHA:

Mom . . . you alright?

BETH:

Mama's real good, Baby girl. Don't worry about me none. I just need to call some family members and let them know what done happened here tonight is all. (They both come over and the trio embrace center stage. The children break the embrace and exit. Beth remains c stage and look skyward.) Lord, I tell you the truth, it's just like the pastor said this morning in church—life is too short, death is too certain, hell is too hot and eternity is too long to fool around with your soul. (Goes over, flops down in a chair, takes a deep breath. Hangs up the phone up quickly and goes over and picks up Saul's pistol. Brandishes it as he did days earlier. Stops and looks at the pistol very stoically and emotionally. Very slowly and deliberately brandishes it once more and slowly lowers it back to its original position on the table.) Too long. Too short. Too certain. Too hot . . . to play around with your soul. (Exits. LIGHTS.)

FINAL CURTAIN